A Key to

A Key to Balthasar

Hans Urs von Balthasar on Beauty, Goodness, and Truth

Aidan Nichols, OP

Baker Academic

a division of Baker Publishing Group
Grand Rapids, Michigan

© 2011 Aidan Nichols, OP

Published by Baker Academic
a division of Baker Publishing Group
P.O. Box 6287, Grand Rapids, MI 49516-6287
www.bakeracademic.com

ISBN: 978-0-8010-3974-4

First published in the UK 2011 by
Darton, Longman and Todd Ltd
1 Spencer Court
140 – 142 Wandsworth High Street
London SW18 4JJ

Printed in Great Britain

Library of Congress Cataloging-in-Publication data is on file at the Library of
Congress, Washington, DC.

Contents

Foreword

I started reading Balthasar at the very beginning of my study of theology. In many ways, this was trying to run before one could walk. I didn't have the background or the tools to do proper justice to what I read. I should really have recognised that the demands of the ideas were too much for me. I was certainly aware that only by very painful plodding could I make out anything at all of what was going on in the German text. In those far off days (I am speaking of 1970), one had to plunge into the German original unless one was going just to stick with some of Balthasar's essays or shorter and easier books, like, for example, his study of St Thérèse of Lisieux – actually, quite an important one because it is where he tells what a *theological* biography of a saint should be, and why.

The German original of Balthasar's *Glory*, in all its multi-volume massiveness, was put into my hands quite out of the blue, by a former fellow-undergraduate at Christ Church, Oxford, a man of singular generosity of heart (and, evidently, purse!). I remember gazing at the handsome maroon books on my shelf at Blackfriars in St Giles' Street and wondering whether I should ever penetrate their mysteries. Why, in my very amateur way, did I persevere?

We were living in something of an ice-age for Catholic theology. At any rate in the Thames Valley, a spiritual chill had descended in place of the Pentecostal warmth the Second Vatican Council was supposed to have communicated. The theology we heard most about (not that our Dominican teachers were necessarily enthusiasts for it) was critical theology. It was what would now be called theology practiced in terms of a 'hermeneutic of discontinuity'. At its worst, it was angrily dismissive of the theology of the past. At its best, it offered a minimal, pared-down version of the older content. The Fathers were sunk in Hellenism, St Thomas ruined by rationalism, later writers oscillated between piety and the seminary manual. There was not much to be expected in all this for 'modern man'.

At least one modern man found there wasn't much for him in critical theology either. Surely, this humanistic make-over couldn't be all that Catholic Christianity had to offer the life of the spirit, the life of the believing intelligence? It was to try to get closer to the sheer spiritual greatness of the revelation to which the art of the Church and the historic liturgies bore witness that I (and, I am sure, others) turned towards Balthasar. That was why I continued to look longingly at those mute maroon covers.

Something I have discovered over the years is that if you want to understand something, the best way is often to teach it, or, failing that, to write about it. I have tried to write about most of Balthasar's corpus, from his early studies of philosophy and art to his famous 'trilogy', and beyond that, the remainder of his theological output which precedes, accompanies and (in the case of a small number of texts) comes after that trilogy. Here, however, I want to do something different – based mainly on material I first put together for a course of lectures at the John Paul II Institute in Melbourne (Australia) some few years ago.

The aim is to provide a key (please note the indefinite article!) to Balthasar by identifying some basic words that structure his trilogy – the three-part project which, on any version of his achievement, occupies a central place in what he was trying to do. Although it is freer than the strict expository style I adopted in the five more substantial books on his corpus I published earlier (Chapter Four is the most disciplined in this respect), I hope it captures much that is useful in what Balthasar sought to say. The trilogy turns on beauty, goodness, and truth. It was because Balthasar's work struck me as all three of entrancingly beautiful, encouraging to goodness and expressive of truth, that I did not give up an effort I have found, as a priest and preacher, enormously worthwhile. And I should add that, while, no doubt, other Fathers, doctors, and approved intellectual luminaries in the Church have said some things better, Balthasar, by his admiration for his predecessors and his manifold use of them, made us love them too and so rediscover the whole Tradition.

Blackfriars, Cambridge
Feast of SS Philip and James, 2010

Chapter One

Key-word 'Being':

Balthasar and the Transcendentals

Introduction

Balthasar's theology has as its universally recognised centre-piece his theological trilogy: in English, *The Glory of the Lord*, *Theo-drama* and *Theo-logic*[1]. Those three works need to be placed all together on one's book-shelf – which will have to be a stout one to bear their weight! Some recent German writers call *The Glory of the Lord* the 'Theo-aesthetics', and while that is not the title Balthasar chose, it does bring out the way each of these multi-volume efforts is parallel to the others. His theological trilogy, perhaps the high-point of twentieth-century Catholic theology, revolves around three 'transcendental' qualities or determinations of being: the beautiful, the good, and the true.

'Transcendental', as used by Balthasar, is not a word that need frighten us. It means, simply, *universal*, in the sense of that which is not confined by but goes beyond (*transcends*) all particular categories. To approach these matters, we can start from a very basic point. Balthasar thinks that despite (or is it owing to?) our human perspective, we can succeed in grasping being, the bed-rock of reality, and that we can do so by way of the senses – seeing, touching, hearing, scenting, tasting – these humble, but also fascinating, faculties which, surely, delight more than they repel. We come into intellectual contact with being, helped by the senses, in and through particular, concrete things. Philosophically, then, Balthasar is an *epistemological optimist* – he holds that our powers of knowing are reliable. And likewise he is an *ontological realist* – he considers that those powers give us access to things as they really are: participations, varying in scope and intensity, in being itself. And he would add, along with all metaphysicians in the Judaeo-Christian tradition, the Ground and Source of such being is God. So the activity of our seemingly lowly senses goes together with access to comprehensive, and even ultimate, reality. As he wrote:

> *No metaphysics of Being as such and its*
> *transcendental qualities can be separated from*
> *concrete experience, which is always of the senses.*
> *'The True', the disclosure of Being in its totality,*
> *only becomes visible where a particular thing is*
> *adjudged true. The goodness of Being is only*
> *visible where one meets with some good thing*
> *which both brings 'the Good' near and – through*
> *its finitude, fragility and relative 'badness' –*
> *causes it to retreat again. And we know that*
> *there is beauty from the sensuous experience*
> *which presents and withdraws it, reveals and*
> *again conceals it, evanescent, in myriad layers ...*[2]

Balthasar's approach can be contrasted here with the Kant-inspired methodology of subject-oriented philosophical humanism and, in the Catholic context, the influential movement of philosophical theology known as 'Transcendental Thomism'. These have it in common that they begin their epistemological reflections by examining human subjectivity from within – on the basis of what has been called the 'I'-'I' relationship.[3] Balthasar, however, puts the human subject – and that by virtue of its created nature – in immediate relation with the truth that lies outside itself. The self-conscious subject exists, knowing that he or she exists as just such a unique subject, yes. But this is always *in relation to other manifestations of being.*

Indeed, our first conscious recognition of ourselves, our 'I', is, so Balthasar suggests, through our relation with another: namely, the human parent. As he put it in 'A Résumé of my Thought' (a useful essay indeed for so prolific and sometimes prolix an author):

[M]an exists only in dialogue with his neighbour.
The infant is brought to consciousness of himself only
by love, by the smile of his mother. In that encounter
the horizon of all unlimited being opens itself for him,
revealing four things to him: (1) that he is one in love
with the mother, even in being other than his mother,
therefore all being is one; (2) that love is good,
therefore all being is good; (3) that love is true, therefore
all being is true; (4) that love evokes joy, therefore all
being is beautiful.[4]

We can take it that in these remarks Balthasar is moving within an intellectual space which may broadly be described as in the tradition of St Thomas Aquinas, the 'universal and common doctor' of the Catholic Church. The passage presumes as its background a participation metaphysic of the sort St Thomas used increasingly in his work, albeit refining it in the process. Thus a Dutch Thomas interpreter from the contemporary 'School of Utrecht' can remark:

Insofar as a creature is a being by participation
and derives its being from God who is essential
being, it is also good by participation, and by an
intrinsic form which is a likeness of God's
essential goodness.[5]

When we compare this quotation from the rather celebrated one from Balthasar about the mother's smile, we notice that Balthasar is working with a wider number of transcendentals: not just one (the transcendental 'goodness') but four. As he writes in his essay 'Revelation and the Beautiful':

The light of the transcendentals, unity, truth,
goodness and beauty, a light at one with the light
of philosophy, can only shine if it is undivided.[6]

Beauty, goodness, unity, and truth are, in the last analysis, inseparable. I should add what the alert reader may well come to notice: among these qualities, *unity* seems the poor relation in Balthasar's account, or at any rate it does not get, so far as explicit treatment is concerned, an equal share of the cake. Balthasar's principal theological work is a trilogy – on divine beauty, divine goodness, divine truth, and the modes in which these are manifested in creation and salvation. It is not, then, a tetralogy; there is no corresponding series of volumes inspired by the transcendental 'unity'. But this is not because Balthasar is uninterested in that topic. It is, rather, because his quite passionate interest in the topic takes an unexpected guise. The transcendental we call 'unity' finds expression in the holism of reality – and this for Balthasar is true above all of the holistic character of the reality that is Christian revelation. This is the real at its most comprehensively complete. In this sense, each of the works in the trilogy is concerned with *unum*, 'the one', since, as the German Balthasar commentator Thomas Schumacher writes, 'in its own special perspective, each part of the trilogy makes explicit (in a way both philosophical and theological) reality as a whole'[7]. Furthermore, so we may add, the transcendental we call 'unity' shows itself in the manner in which beauty, goodness, and truth, wherever found, are indivisibly *one*.

How do we know? Thomas, for his part, has an adage to the effect that, *whatever* is known – and that would include, then, a grasp of the transcendentals – is known according to the knower's capacity. Balthasar certainly accepts that, in the individual subject's perception of the being of things, the degree of understanding found will turn on certain subjective conditions being met within that individual. But while such a view – even in St Thomas – could be construed as offering an opening to Idealism as represented by Kant, what decisively demarcates Balthasar's thought from Idealism is his insistence that the 'first prerequisite for understanding is to accept what is given just as it offers itself'[8]. That is how he puts it in the opening volume of *The Glory of the Lord*, his study of the beautiful. Every reality furnishes proof of its existence by virtue of what he calls:

*the objective evidence that emerges and sheds its
light from the phenomenon itself, and not the sort
of evidence that is recognised in the process of
satisfying the subject's needs.*[9]

Nor is it by accident that it is in his theological aesthetics that
Balthasar makes this point. One of the special functions of the
beautiful, in his view, is to make us aware that in knowing we
receive more than we project. Reality is more fundamentally a
gift to us than it is a construction by us. How could we be amazed
by being in its beauty if what we call knowledge of the world
tells us more about us than it does about it – more about
ourselves than about the world in all its variegated splendour?

We exist, then (we may safely conclude), in relation to a
world of things which by their presence make themselves known
to us. The human mind lies open not just to a series of finitudes
but also to the infinite unlimitedness of being (in the singular)
thus made known in beings (in the plural). Through our awareness of finitude – our own finitude, and the finitude of the
realities around us, we are also aware by that very token that,
while all things are limited, being is not. In calling something
finite, we are implicitly placing it in the context of the infinite.
That is a further nuance it is important to note about this 'being'
business. Indeed, Balthasar calls such awareness of finitude in
the face of unlimited being: 'the source of all the religious and
philosophical thought of humanity'[10].

The transcendentals themselves

So far we have identified Balthasar's approach to epistemology
and ontology in its most basic tenor. Now we must take a further
step and look rather more closely at the transcendentals themselves. Every existing thing, sheerly by virtue of its existence,
shares in being and in the so-called 'transcendental' qualities of
being: unity, truth, goodness and beauty – so called because (as
already intimated) these qualities occur in different ways and to
different degrees in many kinds of things, thus 'transcending'

the normal categories by which we divide up the world. Or, in Balthasar's own words in 'Résumé':

> *The One, the Good, the True, and the Beautiful,*
> *these are what we call the transcendental*
> *attributes of Being, because they surpass all the*
> *limits of essences and are co-extensive with*
> *Being.*[11]

Since they characterise all being, they should be considered as belonging together in an inseparable mutual co-inherence. To cite Balthasar's 'Résumé' again:

> *As the transcendentals run through all Being,*
> *they must be interior to each other: that which*
> *is truly true is also truly good and beautiful*
> *and one.*[12]

And he goes on to explain that this is – to a degree – verified in our own experience:

> *A being appears, it has an epiphany: in that it is*
> *beautiful and makes us marvel. In appearing it*
> *gives itself, it delivers itself to us: it is good. And*
> *in giving itself up, it speaks itself, it unveils itself:*
> *it is true.*[13]

Contact, then, with concrete essences in their existence generates an experience of the transcendentals. This is hardly surprising. Owing to their commonality, the transcendentals set up networks of connexion between the objects that participate in them. 'To exist' means to belong to the transcendental network of being and thus to be related to all other things. Indeed, it could be said that if being, with its transcendental determinations, were *not* shared by all things, then philosophically speaking every object would be absolutely distinct from every other, and we would not live in a *world* – a common universe – at all.

For Balthasar, following in this a long tradition in Thomistic thought, the transcendentals constitute a bridge between the Source of all Being, God, and the finite existents that compose the creation. They are, so to speak, living bonds between God and the world.

> *Since the transcendental properties of being are*
> *supracategorical, they must be, Balthasar argues,*
> *predicable to both divine and worldly being.*[14]

At the same time, following the cue of the Fourth Lateran Council (1215), and an old Jesuit mentor, Erich Przywara: though the transcendentals of created being serve as analogues for divine Being, the difference between created being and uncreated Being is always greater than any similarity.[15] This, however, does not prevent Balthasar from writing in his essay 'Revelation and the Beautiful':

> *Created being would not be an image and, in*
> *Thomas's expression, 'outflow' of the sovereign*
> *and living God if its transcendentals were static*
> *properties, clear and evident to our view, or if,*
> *despite their immanence in all contingent beings,*
> *they did not have something of the freedom and*
> *mysterious depths of God's decision to reveal*
> *himself.*[16]

This rather riddling passage – about how the transcendentals are not 'static' but in some way have something about them of God's own freedom – hints at two further facets of Balthasar's teaching on the transcendental determinations of being.[17] First, the transcendentals somehow point us to the dynamic life going on for ever within God. It seems likely that Balthasar has in mind here the notion that the transcendentals are joined in continuous reciprocal interpenetration – the good, the beautiful, and the true inhering in each other in unity. Given Balthasar's overall theological vision, I do not think it excessive to consider that shimmering interplay a shadow of the eternal interchange in the Holy Trinity. For in the triune Creator, the Persons exist through the mutually related way they possess the divine essence in their relations with each other. Or, as Balthasar himself puts it, there must be, in this interpenetration of the transcendentals:

> *some analogy with the divine Being, from whom*
> *all created beings originate and who, we surmise,*
> *is the supreme reality that pervades all finitudes.*[18]

And secondly, in that somewhat enigmatic passage from 'Revelation and the Beautiful', there is also the suggestion of a relation between the transcendentals and divine revelation. That creatures, and notably human creatures, participate in the transcendentals in only a partial, fragmentary way, despite the human openness to the infinitude of being, implies something of the unfinished nature of creation. Only with the further self-gift of God in revelation in history – supreme evidence of the divine freedom – will the openness to the infinite the human creature possesses find its fulfilment. Writing specifically of beauty, Balthasar declares:

> *An apparent enthusiasm for the beautiful is mere*
> *idle talk when divorced from the sense of a*
> *divine summons to change one's life.*[19]

The transcendentals, so Balthasar will maintain, serve as the structure that is needed if man is to perceive and respond to that divine revelation – itself Cross-and-Resurrection-centred – which brings creation to completion. There is a 'sphere of openness', he writes, where our created being can be drawn into communion with God's uncreated being, and this

> *sphere of openness contains, hidden and*
> *unfinished, the goods of salvation: peace in*
> *God, beatitude and transfiguration, victory*

> *over sin, paradise present though concealed,*
> *all that the beautiful consoles us with ...*

Through the transcendentals we can have a foretaste or anticipation of a fulfilment that is itself 'wholly other' since it consists in the self-gift to creatures of God himself.[20] By the end of this short book, I hope readers will have a reasonable grasp of how that is so.

What Balthasar wanted, then, was a philosophy, and ultimately a theology, that started from the analogy of being (the limited but real comparison we can make between created being and its Uncreated font or source). He did not, however, as sometimes in Neo-Thomism, understand this as abstract being, 'common being', being as we think of it by abstraction from its supreme qualities, a theme which recurs in Transcendental Thomism albeit in a very different manner. Instead, he would begin from an analogy of being *as being is encountered concretely in the transcendentals.*

A first conclusion

Balthasar tends to criticise contemporary theology, whether conservative or more innovatory, for failing to view creation and revelation sufficiently holistically. The form taken by creation and revelation can only be grasped when creation and revelation are viewed as they were designed to be viewed: not as fragments but as a symphonic whole. *Die Wahrheit ist symphonisch*, 'truth is symphonic', is one of Balthasar's favourite expressions.[21] This is pertinent to the transcendentals, just as they, the transcendentals, are extremely pertinent to it, to Balthasar's maxim. It is the human capacity for perceiving the whole that grants us the possibility of experiencing being in its inherently beautiful truth and goodness. How that works out, in the service of an account of the triune God, Creator and Redeemer, revealed in Jesus Christ, will become more apparent in the trio of essays that follow.

[1]   *The Glory of the Lord. A Theological Aesthetic* (San Francisco, Ignatius, 1982–1991); *Theo-drama. Theological Dramatic Theory* (San Francisco, Ignatius, 1988–1998); *Theo-logic. Theological Logical Theory* (San Francisco, Ignatius, 2000–2005). One should also mention here his *Epilogue* to the trilogy (San Francisco, Ignatius, 2004). The present 'key' is not a stage-by-stage commentary, for which see my own little trilogy: *The Word has been Abroad. A Guide through Balthasar's Aesthetics* (Edinburgh, T. & T. Clark, 1998); *No Bloodless Myth. A Guide through Balthasar's Dramatics* (Edinburgh, T. & T. Clark, 2000), and *Say it is Pentecost. A Guide through Balthasar's Logic* (Edinburgh, T. & T. Clark, 2001). This little book is more impressionistic, as well as containing some responses to the more frequently lodged objections to Balthasar's work.

[2]   'Transcendentality and Gestalt', *Communio* 11 (1984), pp. 29–39, and here at p. 34. All books and articles cited are by Balthasar unless otherwise indicated.

[3]   To avoid possible confusion, it should be noted that, as a result of the influence of Kant, the word 'transcendental' has undergone a sea-change in much modern philosophy. In Kantian circles, 'transcendental philosophy' means that philosophical method which would establish the conditions of possibility for subjective experience. More widely, in philosophical schools not especially interested in the medieval achievement, 'transcendental' may denote the question of the foundation of thought, i.e. the search for that which an intellectual affirmation of reality cannot do without.

[4]   'A Résumé of my Thought', *Communio* 15 (1988), pp. 468–473, and here at pp. 470–471. If we think that is a rather hasty progression of thought, we may be reassured to learn that, beginning from the same starting-point, a 'suasion' or quasi-argument for the existence of God has been worked out in a more step-by-step manner by the American Jesuit John Michael McDermott, whose early work was on the French Jesuit interpreter of St Thomas, Pierre Rousselot – also admired by Balthasar. See J. M. McDermott, 'Faith, Reason and Freedom', *Irish Theological Quarterly* 67 (2002), pp. 307–332.

[5]   R. A. te Velde, *Participation and Substantiality in Thomas Aquinas* (Leiden, Brill, 1995), p. 34.

[6]   'Revelation and the Beautiful', in *Explorations in Theology I. The Word made Flesh* (San Francisco, Ignatius, 1989), pp. 95–126 and here at p. 107. The German original antedates *Herrlichkeit*, being published as early as 1959. The theological aesthetics began to come out in the original German in 1961.

[7]   T. Schumacher, *Perichorein. Zur Konvergenz von Pneumatologik und Christologik in Hans Urs von Balthasars theodramatischen Entwurf einer Theologik* (Munich, Institut zur Förderung der Glaubenslehre, 2007), p. 16.

[8]   *The Glory of the Lord. A Theological Aesthetics I. Seeing the Form* (San Francisco, Ignatius, 1982), p. 467.

[9]   Ibid., p. 464.

[10] 'A Résumé of my Thought', art. cit., p. 469.

[11] Ibid., p. 471.

[12] Ibid., pp. 471–472.

13 Ibid., p. 472.

14 S. van Erp, *The Art of Theology. Hans Urs von Balthasar's Theological Aesthetics and the Foundations of Theology* (Leuven, Peeters, 2004), p. 106.

15 See E. T. Oakes, S. J., 'Erich Przywara and the Analogy of Being', in idem., *Pattern of Redemption. The Theology of Hans Urs von Balthasar* (New York, Continuum, 1994), pp. 15–44. Father Oakes' book is a very sophisticated and elegant, as well as scholarly and thoughtful, study and can be unreservedly recommended to the reader.

16 'Revelation and the Beautiful', art. cit., p. 111.

17 Balthasar does not simply, then, *reproduce* Thomasian – or any other high mediaeval – thinking on the *transcendentia* (later, *transcendentalia*). See M. Lochbrunner, 'Hans Urs von Balthasars Trilogie der Liebe', *Forum katholische Theologie* 11 (1995), pp. 161–181, and especially p. 174.

18 'Earthly Beauty and Divine Glory', *Communio* 10 (1983), pp. 202–206, and here at p. 202.

19 'Revelation and the Beautiful', art. cit., p. 107.

20 Ibid., pp. 111–112.

21 Giving its title to a work translated as *Truth is Symphonic. Aspects of Christian Pluralism* (San Francisco, Ignatius, 1987), in which see especially pp. 7–9.

Chapter Two

Key-word 'Form':

Balthasar and the Beautiful

The place of beauty

Balthasar was deeply opposed to the separation of the beautiful
from the true and the good. The idea of beauty, he lamented, has
been reduced to that of a merely this-worldly aesthetics, with
baleful consequences for Christian faith and morals. Beauty's
separation from the other transcendentals, and the consequent
rise of what Balthasar terms the 'aestheticisation' of the beautiful,[22] is at least partly responsible, he thinks, for the inability of
people to pray and contemplate. The notion of the sheer beauty
of the divine Being has disappeared. The severance of beauty
from goodness and truth also helps to explain the perceived
reduction of the moral order to a self-centred relativism, and the
retrenchment of the metaphysical order to a materialism placed
at the service of either technology or psychology or both. The
final upshot of all this, he predicts, will be incapacity for either
faith or love.[23] Unfashionably, Balthasar holds that, in the modern Western epoch, the Church has become the guardian of
metaphysics. We live in a period when 'things are deprived of
the splendour reflected from eternity'[24]. In our time, only an
orthodox Christian mind and heart can bridge the gap between,
on the one hand, an acosmic spirituality – a religiosity concerned
merely with salvation in some other realm, private, interior,
extra-mundane, and, on the other hand, a present world con-
signed to domination by positivists for whom all that exists is
only organised matter. Revelation can be a therapy for a metaphysical malaise that has, at the moment, no other medicine

available. Tutored by revelation, the orthodox believer can show people how once again to experience the cosmos as what Balthasar terms 'the revelation of an infinity of grace and love'[25]. In the course of the eighty or one hundred years before Balthasar was writing, imaginative writers like Gerard Manley Hopkins, in England, and, in France, Paul Claudel and Charles Péguy managed precisely this, as had in Austria, *qua* composer of music, Wolfgang Amadeus Mozart a century before them. They showed it was possible. And so they gave us marching orders for what we in our turn should be doing – 'all proportions guarded', as the French say, not all of us can be great creative artists – as Christians who reflect on the revelation given them and wish to apply its benefits to the surrounding culture.

More widely, in Balthasar's analysis, there must be a reunion of philosophy and theology, and, within theology, a reunion of spirituality and dogmatic thought, if there is to be for Western man – who is now for many purposes global man – a recovery of the sense of the integrity of being, in its co-constitutive transcendent and immanent dimensions. Thus in the first part of his trilogy, which he called a 'theological aesthetics', Balthasar sets himself the task of trying to perceive the objective form of revelation, in creation and in Jesus Christ, in all its splendid, harmonious and symphonic fullness.

What are 'theological aesthetics'?

What, then, does Balthasar mean by 'theological aesthetics'? It is important to get clear from the outset that he does not intend to confine himself to a consideration of the beauty of the created world – whether, with antiquity, we have in mind there the harmony of the cosmic order, or whether, in the spirit of European Romanticism, we are more struck by the terrible but wonderful power of nature. Without excluding such considerations, the defining question of theological aesthetics goes beyond them – as it must if it is to include in its purview not only creation but salvation. For Balthasar, that defining question runs: How can the revelation of God's sovereign grace be perceived in the world?

In his use of the phrase 'theological aesthetics', Balthasar gives the 'aesthetics' component two co-essential meanings. The first of these is indebted to Immanuel Kant, who used the word frequently enough in his *Critique of Judgment*, which is itself an essay in philosophical aesthetics albeit of the limited sort that Kant, on his own presuppositions in epistemology and ontology, felt able to write. 'Aesthetics' considers the part played at the higher levels of our experience by the human senses, of which sight has often been singled out as the most noble. So '*theological* aesthetics' will consider the part played by the senses – with their associated powers of memory and imagination – in the awareness of God. Balthasar invokes this meaning of the phrase in relation to, above all, the series of revelatory events and processes which culminated in the appearance of Christ. In Christ, his eternal Word or Son now come on earth, God made himself – as the First Letter of St John insists – a sensuous Object, being seen, heard, touched.[26] Indeed, thanks to the assumption of human nature by the Logos at the Incarnation, a woman (we call her, accordingly, the *Theotokos*, the 'God-bearer') felt him growing in her body. In the opening volume of *The Glory of the Lord*, Balthasar stresses the way the divine 'form' that is made available to human perception in Jesus Christ is mediated by the historical record (the Gospels and other New Testament writings), but also by the Liturgy and Christian experience. In various ways, a number of which he explores, the human imagination has been seized by this central figure of revelation – this (in Latin) *figura*, this (in German) *Gestalt*, this (in both English and German) *F/form*, which is close enough to another Latin word for it: *forma*.

Still on the first meaning of the phrase 'theological aesthetics': when Balthasar embarked on this project, many readers seemed to have had difficulty in getting hold of what he was saying. But really, his concept of the aesthetic perception should not perplex a readership in any way familiar with the *res Christiana*, 'the Christian thing'. Take, for example, what G. K. Chesterton has to say on the subject in his celebrated cameo study *St Thomas Aquinas*. In the passage I have in mind, he is talking about the difference the Incarnation makes, or should make, to the way we evaluate the importance of the senses. In Christian theology, wrote Chesterton

> *[t]here really was a new reason for regarding the*
> *senses, and the sensations of the body, and the*
> *experiences of the common man, with a reverence*
> *at which great Aristotle would have stared, and*
> *no man in the ancient world could have begun to*
> *understand. The Body was no longer what it was*
> *when Plato and Porphyry and the old mystics had*
> *left it for dead. It had hung upon a gibbet. It had*
> *risen from a tomb. It was no longer possible for the*
> *soul to despise the senses, which had been the*
> *organs of something that was more than man. Plato*
> *might despise the flesh but God had not despised it.*
> *The senses had truly become sanctified; as they are*
> *blessed one by one at a Catholic baptism. 'Seeing is*
> *believing' was no longer the platitude of a mere*
> *idiot, or common individual, as in Plato's world; it*
> *was mixed up with real conditions of real belief.*[27]

So much, then, for the first meaning of 'aesthetics' in the term 'theological aesthetics': it signifies, quite simply, having to do with the senses.

The second way in which Balthasar uses the term 'theological aesthetics' is to denote a study of beauty – more especially an account of beauty as a transcendental determination of being, and most especially of all an exploration of the revealed correlate of beauty which is, so Balthasar held, the *glory* of God.

Not all the Scholastics had treated *pulchrum*, 'the beautiful', explicitly as a transcendental[28], but the conviction gradually settled on the Thomist school that it is – just as much as truth and goodness or the remaining transcendental which Balthasar never used to structure a distinct theological treatise: unity. Thus for a mid-twentieth century Thomist, Jacques Maritain, beauty is the 'splendour of being and of all the transcendentals re-united'[29]. On this presupposition, we might describe beautifully formed objects as in-gatherings and out-pourings of that 'splendour'. In Balthasar's case, the most important of the key terms in the *first* use of 'aesthetics', namely 'form', recurs in the *second* way Balthasar uses the term. Form is just as important to an understanding of beauty as it is to an account of how reality is presented to us by the senses. Again, some people confess themselves bemused by what Balthasar means by the word 'form', which owes something to Goethe but rather more to Aquinas.[30] But here, once more, is what Chesterton had to say in his little book on St Thomas:

> *'Formal' in Thomist language means actual or possessing the real decisive quality that makes a thing itself. Roughly, when [Thomas] describes a thing as made out of Form and Matter, he very rightly recognises that Matter is the more mysterious and indefinite and featureless element; and that what stamps anything with its identity is its Form.*

And Chesterton goes on to say in this same passage:

> *Every artist knows that the form is not superficial but fundamental; that the form is the foundation. Every sculptor knows that the form of the statue is not the outside of the statue, but rather the inside of the statue; even in the sense of the inside of the sculptor. Every poet knows that the sonnet-form is not only the form of the poem, but the poem.*

And Chesterton concludes, rather peremptorily perhaps:

> *No modern critic who does not understand what the mediaeval Schoolman meant by form can meet the mediaeval Schoolman as an intellectual equal.*[31]

Like Chesterton and indeed Maritain, Balthasar is thinking of natural forms as well as humanly shaped ones. A relatively straightforward summary of what he has in mind might run something like this. The perceptible form of an object is the expression, under particular conditions, of its metaphysical form – its essence or nature. We are glad when a perceptual form is rich, clear, and expressive because we feel that it lays open the object to us, even though we may also feel there is more in the thing's nature than appears in this or that single expression.

From here we can go one step further. Something's nature, surely, is itself one expression of the inherent possibilities of being at large. So when, in appreciating the clear, rich, expressive sensuous form, we also look through it to the nature of the thing in question, through that again we look to what one student of Balthasar's aesthetics has called 'the vast ocean of formal fertility which is the mystery of being'[32]. The form of a thing may tell us more than just about itself. It may also tell us something about the world in which it is situated, about the universe.

The clarity of form in Balthasar's aesthetics can usefully be contrasted with Descartes' equally strong emphasis on 'clarity' in his philosophy of mind. Descartes was in love with what he called 'clear and distinct ideas'. Balthasar's concept of clarity, however, is taken from Thomas, for whom clarity – radiance – is one of the essential traits of the beautiful, along with proportion and integrity. This is a very different sort of 'brightness'. The brightness of the beautiful is something that overwhelms us, impelling us and enabling us to enter further into the depths of being than the unaided intelligence can venture. And whereas the Cartesian 'idea' is, in Scholastic terms, an intuited potential essence – something that may or may not be the case about the world, the Thomistic 'radiance' is expressed by a form actually enacting its own existence, its being-in-act.

We could explain the meaning of the second component in 'theological aesthetics' as an intersection of two axes: 'vertical' and 'horizontal' (not exactly exhilarating language, but it is

handy). For Balthasar, the dimensions of the beautiful are 'verti-
cally', an infinite depth of splendour, which, 'horizontally', is
expressed in a materially graspable extension of form. The
beautiful unifies – on the one hand – the definitely shaped form
of something present, something on which the mind can come to
rest, with – on the other hand – an endless sea of radiant
intelligibility in which the mind can move without limitation.
The beautiful is, as he would put it, the meeting-place of finite
form with infinite light.

Balthasar seems to expand the Scholastic teaching on *pulchrum* by marrying it with the notion of the 'sublime', an idea
the late-eighteenth-century Romantic authors found, or thought
they found, in the ancients. The sublime reminds people that
ontological beauty is a mystery whose inner momentum can
never fully be grasped.[33] Unlike the Romantics, however,
Balthasar is always careful not to allow 'sublimity' to dissolve
forms into a general sea of being, where objects lose their
outlines and coalesce.

The centrality of Christ in aesthetics

Where the perceptual object in question is Jesus Christ, the real
object thus presented to us is not just one of the possibilities of
created being. Owing to the Incarnation, the object here presented through beautiful form is not merely human being but in a
direct and plenary way divine Being itself. In this unique
instance, then, the sensuous appearance is loaded with the endless significance and inherent authority of the divine. In this
particular case, accordingly, 'beauty' will also be called 'glory'
as well, for appearance charged with the inexhaustible significance and inherent authority of the divine is a plausible first stab
at defining what the Judaeo-Christian Scriptures mean by 'the
glory of the Lord'.

Balthasar's aesthetics begin humbly, at the level of sense
perception, but ultimately they investigate the meaning and
content of encounter with the glory of God. The form of revela-

tion is the main theme of Balthasar's theological aesthetics because it is 'the glorious evidence of divine agency in the world'[34]. God, of course, is not part of the world. He cannot be ranged among the many things that happen to exist (a good Thomistic point: God is not in any genus of being, any type of thing). This does not mean, however, that God fails to attain to form. Surely we should say, rather, that *God is that to which all form fails to attain*. We can call him, with Balthasar, not 'non-form' but 'Super-form'.

In speaking of God as 'Super-form', Balthasar offers his own theologically aesthetic version of the Thomistic claim that the human creature has a natural desire for the vision of God. Translated into theologically aesthetic terms, this reads: we humans desire to find a perceivable form that transcends our powers, and in that way to transcend ourselves by knowing ourselves to be thus transcended. For this reason, the contemplation of God is, as the mystics show, not only dark and baffling but also a cause of joy for us.

To search out the beautiful is to explore, then, not only the formal possibilities of being but also the possibilities of human feeling-response in the face of the forms that being takes. It has, therefore, both an objective and a subjective side to it (we shall look at this more closely in a moment). Notice meanwhile how Balthasar is *not* saying that perception of anything beautiful should be regarded as equivalent to an act of recognition of God. What he *is* saying is twofold. First, for those who have some awareness of God as the Source of all being, beauty acquires ontological depth. Such people can develop a habit of seeing the world as transparent to God. That is highly relevant to belief in creation. Secondly, and even more importantly, the events of salvation history – where God is active, presenting himself for contemplation – show the divine to have its own style of manifestation, and we must learn to register its impress. That is highly relevant to belief in the Incarnation. In the biblical revelation, the self-disclosure of God comes to a climax in Jesus Christ. As the centre of Scripture, Christ unifies Old Testament and New

Testament in a single form. Once seen as such, he can *also* be
recognised as the centre of creation: the One who brings genesis
and apocalypse, the original creation and its eschatological
fulfilment, into a single form likewise.[35] In 'Revelation and the
Beautiful', Balthasar draws attention to the need for holism
these affirmations entail:

> *The historical revelation is moulded throughout into*
> *a single structure, so that the person contemplating it*
> *perceives, through the relationships and proportion of*
> *its various parts, the divine rightness of the whole. For*
> *however clear and convincing these relationships are,*
> *they are inexhaustible – not only in the practical sense,*
> *because we lack the power to grasp them in their*
> *entirety, but also in principle, because what comes*
> *to light in the structure is something which opens*
> *our minds to the infinite.*[36]

Note, however, that Jesus Christ is the centre of this structure,
not the exclusive content of it. Though Balthasar's vision always
centres on the figure of Christ, he does not follow the great
Protestant Neo-orthodox theologian Karl Barth, for example, in
making Christ's form as God made human the *sole* analogue
between God and the world. Balthasar states plainly that it is
impossible to understand beauty as supernatural revelation without first experiencing beauty naturally, in creation.[37] Still, perhaps the best argument for the existence of the transcendentals is
their capacity to infuse the human community with shared
meanings where goodness, truth and beauty are concerned. And
in this regard, Jesus Christ, whose Gospel has enabled millions
in many ages and cultures to find such meaning, is as it were an
open window on the transcendentals, joining together webs of
human sensibility so that people can apprehend the transcendentals in their full reality.

Of course, Christ is a very unexpected climax to the experience of the beautiful. As Balthasar suggests in his meditation on
the Easter Triduum, *Mysterium Paschale*, the Incarnation is

ordered to the Passion: from the very word 'Go!' its direction is the Cross.[38] In Jesus Christ it will, then, be a strange and terrible beauty that is born. Hence Balthasar's remark in 'Revelation and the Beautiful':

> *For this reason, the glory inherent in God's*
> *revelation, its fulfillment beyond measure of all*
> *possible aesthetic ideas, must perforce remain*
> *hidden from the eyes of all, believers and*
> *unbelievers, though in very various degrees.*[39]

Naturally, Balthasar can hardly say that the glory of God in the life, death and resurrection of Jesus is something *entirely* hidden to *everybody*: in that case, there would be no point in writing a Christ-centred theological aesthetics at all. But there is a point! The Incarnation is the supreme presentation of aesthetic form despite or rather, when seen more deeply, *because of* the Cross. As Balthasar explains:

> *Insofar as the veil over the face of Christ's mystery is*
> *drawn aside, and insofar as the economy of grace*
> *allows, Christian contemplation can marvel, in the*
> *self-emptying of divine love, at the exceeding wisdom,*
> *truth and beauty inherent there. But it is only in this*
> *self-emptying that they can be contemplated, for it is*
> *the source whence the glory contemplated by the*
> *angels and the saints radiated into eternal life ... The*
> *humiliation of the servant only makes the concealed*
> *glory shine more resplendently, and the descent into*
> *the ordinary and commonplace brings out the*
> *uniqueness of him who so abased himself.*[40]

Here is a form than which none more wonderful can be imagined. For the 'ground' that appears in this 'gestalt', above all in the moment of the Cross, is the love that the Trinity is. That statement is the climactic assertion of Balthasarian 'theo-aesthetics'. In the next Chapter, we shall see how, for Balthasar's 'theo-dramatics', two more words need adding to this formulation: the ground that appears in the Christ-form is the love *and freedom* of the triune God.

The unification of human experience by aesthetic form

In his theological aesthetics Balthasar expects human experience to be completed and unified when guided by aesthetic form. To cite once again from 'Revelation and the Beautiful':

> *Everywhere there should be a correspondence*
> *between object and subject; the external*
> *harmony must correspond to a subjective need*
> *and both give rise to a new harmony of a higher*
> *order; subjectivity, with its feeling and*
> *imagination, must free itself in an objective work,*
> *in which it rediscovers itself, in the course of which*
> *… there may be as much self-discovery as*
> *experience of another.*[41]

As that highly original student of Balthasar's work Francesca Aran Murphy has pointed out, Balthasar presupposes, rightly enough, that human beings need rounded patterns through which to shape their experiences and make of them a coherent unity.[42] Our capacity for awareness of such rounded patterns is called *imagination*.[43] Owing to Balthasar's epistemological optimism and ontological realism, the thrust of the imagination for him is towards the real foundation which upholds all such forms. As we have seen, Balthasar employs a realistic metaphysics for which form is a basic principle. In such a metaphysic, beauty will be treated as an objective reality, present both in natural reality and in artistic works and accessible to us through their mediation. For Balthasar (as for anyone else, for that matter), the word 'imagination' denotes a human faculty that eschews the quantitative measuring techniques of the empirical sciences. But for Balthasar (unlike for many other writers), the functioning of imagination can and should be grounded in objective reality. Whereas historic Romanticism was plagued by Idealism, according to which imagination tells us chiefly about our own minds, the matter looks very different when a realist metaphysic is brought into the picture. Symbolic forms, though of our devising, *allow us to gesture toward the inherent reality of things*. The imagination expresses meaning in terms which draw the mind into the world. When a realist metaphysics, recognising the force of imagination, is combined with an orthodox Christology, the vista opened up is transformed again. Now our imaginative penetration of the world finds its response in a form – a supremely rounded pattern – who rises up to meet it from beyond all human powers of exploration, since *this* form – the form of the Word incarnate – discloses God himself, author and archetype of being as a whole. While revealing itself to us from its source in the Uncreated, from what lies beyond the natural world, this form is also an attracting principle that draws out man's effort to unite himself imaginatively with the created, with the natural order found in the cosmos and in human existence.

At one and the same time, then, the shape of this unique form, Jesus Christ, is both congruent with the activity of the human imagination at large, for imagination in general works on what is given in creation, and yet extends infinitely beyond all humanly discerned patterns – and, indeed, beyond the range of creation itself. As Samuel Taylor Coleridge divined, and he was, in this regard, an English forerunner of Balthasar, the highest unity the imagination can conceive is that which joins the finite and the infinite.[44] But as Balthasar stresses with a vigour absent in Coleridge, this joining is supremely carried out by God himself in assuming human nature into unity with his divine Word.

The deficiencies of modern theological culture

As Balthasar was aware, much modern theology does not honour this claim. Modern theological liberalism characteristically takes as its base the organisation of human experience rather than the objective givens of divine agency impacting on nature and history. Probably Kant is the single greatest culprit here, because he it was who established the quite misleading presupposition that what critical thought considers is merely why we experience the world in the way we do. The situation deteriorates even further with Neo-Kantianism, influential in the German Universities (and notably Marburg – later to host the philosopher Heidegger and the exegete and quasi-theologian Bultmann) around the turn of the nineteenth and twentieth centuries. For Neo-Kantians, the threads binding the Kantian subject to an objective world were attenuated even further. In their view, Kant was hasty in allowing that external sense impressions impinge upon the mind, and misguided in granting the existence of a *noumenon* behind such perceptual presentation, the elusive 'thing in itself'. Such Neo-Kantianism is, it would seem, the philosophical origin of the 'demythologising' movement in Christian theology, and that has been, under whatever name, an enormously influential movement, both academically and in ordinary Church life. It is a movement to which Balthasar was implacably opposed.[45]

Bultmann had regarded all alleged 'knowledge' of reality as mere objectification, projecting onto the largely unknowable a screen of our own culturally generated ideas: such false 'objectivity' must be stripped from the New Testament record. To his mind, the cosmological canvas on which the New Testament writers painted concealed the true message of the Gospel, which is the 'extra-worldly' dependence of the human person on the divine. For Bultmann, the Gospel has to do with my subjective relation to God within my own existence – my relation to him as myself a subject called to shape the meaning of life as I go along, thanks to my own 'existential' decisions, what I choose to regard as 'authentic', as valid 'for me'. Francesca Murphy draws attention to the usefulness of Balthasar's corpus for those seeking to repel the Bultmann-style subversion of revelation-guided thought. Balthasar was clearly right to identify the hazards of granting primacy to what the last Chapter of this study called an 'I'-'I' principle in laying intellectual foundations – rather than the 'I'-world principle where the transcendentals can enter the picture from the very start.

A starting-point in the 'I'-'I' relationship will always prejudice the chances of any presentation of the incarnate Christ as divinity given in and through form. If as philosophers we follow the Kantians (and here is why, unlike most modern thinkers in the German language, Balthasar preferred to Kant the more classically inspired mind-set of Goethe), we abandon the really metaphysical path to God leading as that path does through a substantial, material world – in other words, a world of substances that make themselves known through their forms to human intelligence, mediated by the senses. And when we come to the theology of revelation, where the acting subject is not ourselves but God himself reaching out to us, we shall inevitably, sooner or later, cease to think of God's movement toward us as really mediated by the forms and images, understood as valid for everyone, in which the Bible deals.

This for Balthasar is where appeal to *pulchrum,* the transcendental we call 'the beautiful', can help restore the integrity of a Christologically-given revelation of the God of all being. The significance of the beautiful is that it indicates how an object might be outside us, facing us, and yet at the same time draw us into itself. Of all the transcendentals, the beautiful is the closest to our senses. It is, therefore, more directly present to us than are the other transcendental properties of being. The beautiful is a fully objective property of being, but it is the nature of this property to be communicative, to communicate itself to observers. The beautiful *is* reality under the aspect of form, known as such by imaginative intuition, just as truth is reality as best known through propositions, by the intelligence, and goodness is reality as best known through values, by the moral sense. These ways of knowing refer to the same world manifesting itself in distinct but analogously related ways: as beautiful, true and good respectively. Specifically, the antidote Balthasar would prescribe for the sick theological patient is stored at the centre of his aesthetics where he draws on the Augustinian and mediaeval tradition which ascribed transcendental beauty most especially to the divine Son. In, for example, the *prima pars* of the *Summa Theologiae*, St Thomas explains that Christ has *radiance* through being the Art of the Father, where the Word illuminates the mind that contemplates him. He has *proportion* because he is the fullest likeness of the Father. He has *integrity* because his form *is* the Father's form.[46] And for Aquinas precisely those three qualities – radiance, proportion, integrity – are the hallmarks of the beautiful. St Thomas was speaking of the pre-existent Son, who is with the Father from all eternity. Balthasar, by contrast, wants to apply *pulchrum* to the incarnate Son, precisely in his sensuous as well as intelligible form, a form that is well accommodated to our finitude so that we may grasp it.

But how, we may ask, is this particular doctrine the remedy an ailing theological culture needs? The human yearning for structured intelligibility, the single chief impetus to the making of art, suggested to Balthasar an analogy in art – and notably visual art – for the form and splendour attaching to the transcendent beauty of Christ.[47] Considered as symbols, artworks function within the analogical network of being whose indefinitely extended character we charted in Chapter One. Though they belong to immanent being – the realm of being that is suitably proportioned to the human mind, they also participate in the transcendentals, and thus they have a relation to the transcendent, divine Being that is all creation's source. Aesthetic beauty, we can say, *strives towards* transcendental beauty, and this is a token of its spirituality. Yet aesthetic beauty cannot spiritualise itself. It is ordered to the delight of the embodied human mind of everyman or everywoman – toward the satisfaction of the imagination *as earthed in this world*. It can, then, only *receive* a direction toward the transcendent, and do so, accordingly, *from beyond itself*. The supreme, altogether unified, and yet interior experience the Romantics were looking for is not self-shaped.

Rather, it is shaped by a transcendent and supernatural form. The subject of religious experience, the human self, can be, ought to be, and has been, *re-formed* by its transcendent object. Human experience enters true synthesis through receiving an objective revealed form that brings it to fulfilment. The self becomes re-formed divinely when it lets Christ's archetypal experience form its own.

All instances of the real participate in form in analogically ordered degrees, but that means in unequal degrees. Every beautiful form possesses an openness to the infinite, but some beautiful forms possess this more than others. Beautiful form is heterogeneous, differentiated, qualitatively variable, of more or less significance in terms of focusing the totality of being at large. A snow-crystal, a mango-tree, Michelangelo's statue of King David, the *Aurora Borealis*, St Francis kissing the leper, do this to varying degrees. Every form is a contraction of the totality of being, and some are more contracted than others. This should remind us that it is for *God* to provide the norm by which he will interpret himself (the word-play of 'norm' and 'form' only works in English – and Latin, but Balthasar wants his readers to understand 'authoritative principle' [norm] in aesthetic terms [form]). Only God can fashion a form that could be a comprehensive revelation of himself, the world and our relation to both of these. Balthasar stresses, however, that, though the phenomenon in which God supremely shows himself is indeed overwhelming, it is still a norm that is comprehensible to human modes of perception and knowing, and does not simply override these or lay them to one side. As he puts it in the metaphysics volume of the theological aesthetics:

> ... *if a concept that is fundamental to the Bible*
> *has no kind of analogy in the general*
> *intellectual sphere, and awoke no familiar echo*
> *in the heart of man, it would remain absolutely*
> *incomprehensible and thereby a matter of*
> *indifference. It is only when there is an*

> analogy (*be it only distant*) *between the human*
> *sense of the divine and divine revelation that*
> *the height, the difference and the distance of*
> *that which the revelation discloses may be*
> *measured in God's grace.*[48]

No beauty in the world can be identified with God's glory –
though we might suspect that human personality, where the
being of the world comes to its crown and its varied splendours
(including their relation to God) can be perceived, might be a
special locus for imaging glory (were it not, at any rate, for
moral evil – a rather large obstacle in the way).[49] There is,
however:

> *one concrete historical event in which divine glory*
> *is fully present: in the beauty of the Christ-form.*[50]

Objective and subjective in revelatory 'evidence'

We have said that the aesthetic act always has both an *objective*
and a *subjective* side to it. It is a subject's marvelling appreciation of an object. The absolutely foundational opening volume
of Balthasar's theological aesthetics is governed by this pair of
terms. Divine revelation in Jesus Christ has, in the first place,
subjective evidence. What Balthasar means by 'subjective evidence' here is certainly not vague and conjectural evidence.
Rather, it is *evidence from the side of the human subject*. Divine
revelation in Jesus Christ also has objective evidence. What
Balthasar means by 'objective evidence' is not the only kind of
evidence worth having but, more specifically, *evidence from the*
side of the divine-human object.

Let us take the *subjective evidence* first. It may seem at first
sight disconcerting that Balthasar identifies the subjective evidence for revelation as *faith itself*. Surely faith is a response to
the evidence of revelation: can it be, in that case, itself part of the
evidence? Balthasar holds that, in an important sense, God's
self-revelation is, and can only be, self-authenticating. Faith

accepts its own object on the authority of that object which in this way becomes 'subjective evidence' for it. The classical account of faith as an infused theological virtue – the account found in Thomas – already claimed that our recognition of God is God's own act in us: it is the *inchoatio gloriae*, the 'beginning of glory'.[51] Crucial to the act of faith is a power of apperception experienced as a gift from a source beyond oneself. And yet no such gift – no such grace – is, in Catholic doctrine, irresistible. We have to co-operate. On our part, the grace of faith requires a readiness to receive the light God gives, and a self-surrender to that light. On God's part, faith entails the gift to us of fresh insights, motives, impulses, by which we are gradually shaped into the pattern of Christ as well as granted understanding of that pattern. Behind these statements lies Thomas' account of understanding, and with it ancient Greek philosophy which, thanks chiefly to Aristotle, saw mind as both receptive or 'patient' (passive) and also spontaneous or 'agent' (active). To cite Chesterton's wonderful little Thomas book one last time:

> *The mind is not merely receptive, in the*
> *sense that it absorbs sensations like so much*
> *blotting-paper; on that sort of softness has*
> *been based all that cowardly materialism,*
> *which conceives man as wholly servile to his*
> *environment. On the other hand, the mind is*
> *not purely creative, in the sense that it paints*
> *pictures on the windows and then mistakes*
> *them for a landscape outside. But the mind is*
> *active, and its activity consists in following, so*
> *far as the will chooses to follow, the light outside*
> *that does really shine upon real landscapes.*[52]

A light shines for the mind as well as for the senses when the intellect as agent judges aright the impressions, mental as well as sensuous, that the intellect as patient receives. In the case of faith, this light is a divinely enabled intensification of the intel-

lectual light in which we make our natural judgments. For
Thomas, the light of faith is indeed an anticipation of the light of
glory, the beatific Vision.

In all this, Balthasar's distinctive stress lies on how the light
of faith makes possible, on our own more modest level as
disciples, a certain alignment with the experience of Christ
himself. Balthasar emphasises how archetypal for us as Christians is the experience which Christ himself had in his human
nature of his Father and himself in the Holy Spirit. We come to
know of that uniquely formative experience through the apprehension of Christ found in the New Testament writers – who are
not just a few more authors from the ancient world but inspired
witnesses, or what Greek Christians call 'hagiographs', the
'sacred writers'. The variety of their witness – which for some
scholars undermines the consistency of the figure of Jesus in the
New Testament – Balthasar regards as, on the contrary, vital to
their function. The *varied* appearances of an object to observers
capable of communicating their experience is the only way
something of the object's *fullness* (if it has one) can be transmit-
ted by the witnesses.

In our appreciation of those witnesses, when carried out by
the light of faith, we are to let our own senses and imagination be
disciplined and re-shaped pneumatically – by the action of the
Holy Spirit. Some spiritual authors tell us not to stay on the level
of images, of the imagination. But for Balthasar when, in personal prayer and devotion, we break through to another level
where the sensuous seems to be stripped away, and we go
beyond images, we should not understand that as a happy
victory of the superbly intellectual side of us over the wretchedly
sensuous. Rather, we should understand it as a participation by
precisely that sensuous side of us in the self-emptying of Christ.
For Balthasar, the negative incomprehensibility of God to materially embodied creatures like ourselves is less interesting than
the positive incomprehensibility that derives from the overwhelming greatness of God's triune self-giving or self-humbling
('kenotic') love which the Incarnation and the Paschal Mystery
display.

This brings us, then, to revelation's *objective evidence*. There must also be objective evidence and not *just* subjective, or else Catholics would be fideists – people who think belief can and should proceed without any reference to external legitimating grounds. For Balthasar, the chief objective evidence in Christianity is: Christ Jesus as he is in himself, the Trinitarian Son disclosing in his humanity the hidden tri-unity of divine being. That *includes* what conventional Catholic apologetics has treated as objective evidence for the truth of Jesus' claims – such things as Christ's miracles (above all, his Resurrection), his fulfilment of Old Testament prophecy, the sublimity of his teaching, his moral perfection, and so on. But on Balthasar's understanding of the matter, the Christological objective evidence also *goes beyond* that set of considerations since, after all, they are only *signs* of his Trinitarian identity, not that identity in and of itself.

Now to see Christ in this fuller way for who and what he really is, we must have an unlimited willingness to receive the impress of God's greatness and glory. Here Balthasar's position can be regarded as the exact antithesis to Bultmann's. Bultmann's work belongs to a long line of theological speculation which gradually debilitated the physical and metaphysical texture of its object. For Bultmann, the visually graspable shapes of nature and salvation history do not mediate our approach to God because created being is not constituted from substantial self-transcending forms. Nature and history are not impressed with illustrative form, so God has to be approached in a way that abstracts from all human perceptibility.[53] Balthasar says the contrary. The necessary willingness to receive the impress of God's greatness and glory is mediated in the Church – not least through the variety of her approved theologies, a number of which Balthasar explores in the second and third volumes of *The Glory of the Lord*.[54]

As Balthasar presents it in those volumes and in other essays, theology is a rich and complex activity which at one pole contains the careful logical analysis which explains the faith and

answers heresy ('controversial' theology), and at the other pole –
ultimately, the more important one – embraces the adoring
contemplation of God. The adoring contemplation aspect of
theology may seem something essentially mysteric – typically,
apophatic and imageless, but Balthasar notes how in many of the
great mystics it has gone hand in hand with a capacity for
densely concrete, and in its own way precise, poetic expression.
It is as if the vision of that which is above-and-beyond-form, the
vision of 'Super-form', by its very fascination prompts the
human form-creating powers to move into action on their own
level. The poems of St John of the Cross are a good example, and
indeed Sanjuanist thought is included by Balthasar as one of his
examples of how all great theologies are 'beautiful' through
pointing in some way to the initial vision without which there
would be nothing worthwhile for theologians to analyse in the
manner of a theological logic.[55]

The two volumes of *The Glory of the Lord* devoted to such
historic examples from the work of clerical or lay 'doctors'
(scare-quotes since Balthasar does not confine himself to those
canonically and liturgically so recognised) are not merely illustrative of Balthasar's project or simply preparatory to it. Taken
cumulatively, they are meant to suggest how it is that, without a
theological aesthetics, no theological logic worth its salt can be
written. Unless the content of theology is marvellous, why
indeed should we spend so much time explaining its truth? This
is one important way in which Balthasar's trilogy – aesthetics,
dramatics, logic – hangs together.

Another such way, which relates the aesthetics not to the logic
so much as to the dramatics, is that, for Balthasar, the life of
Christ culminating in the Paschal mystery – the totality of which
constitutes the Christ-form – has all the intelligible beauty of a
drama. The more deeply we penetrate its meaning – ultimately
the task of a theological dramatics – the more this beauty asserts
itself. Theological dramatics, then, requires theological aesthetics. That is why the Church expresses the ugly physical facts of
the Crucifixion not simply as an act of barbaric execution: the

Church presents them as supremely beautiful. Compare the witness of iconography and the exalted language of the Liturgies about the Cross.[56]

The religious 'a priori' and the theological 'a priori'

As the discussion earlier in this Chapter of the grace of faith will already (I hope) have suggested, the light in which we appreciate subjectively the objectivity of the divine epiphany in Jesus Christ is not the same as the intellectual light in which the mind makes natural judgments – even though both of these kinds of illumination are given by God. Despite his dislike of the blood-less abstractions of Transcendental Thomism, Balthasar uses a formula of the sort such Thomism borrowed from Kant so that he can underline the difference he sees here.

In his epistemological writings, Kant had used the Latin logical term '*a priori*' to refer to the way human understanding is structured in advance as it comes to scan the materials of experience. Using this same terminology, it is of great importance to Balthasar to grasp the distinction between what he terms the 'religious *a priori*' in our ordinary human experience and the 'theological *a priori*' in our distinctively Christian experience.

Let us take the religious *a priori* first. The religious *a priori* is our natural participation in the light of God as Creator. That prior structure of human awareness is 'transcendental' in the sense of the word proper to Kant and the – in Kantian perspective, rightly so named – 'Transcendental' Thomists. This sense of the word should be carefully distinguished, then, from the meaning given it by the high mediaevals (see Chapter One of this study, and especially note 2) in whose company Balthasar was more at home.) The religious *a priori* is the 'transcendental' presupposi-tion of the objective vision we can entertain of the divine reality in, and on the occasion of, the natural forms of creation. It is the source of religious experience in general, and includes an intui-tion of the absence as well as the presence of God in all contingent being which, of course, as contingent, finite, imper-

fect, can never entirely mediate the God who is absolute, infinite, perfect. This is how human beings produce symbols and
construct myths about the 'What' and the 'Who' lying beyond all
creation. The religious *a priori* is the source of mytho-poetic
thought in all cultures and periods.

How, then, does the theological *a priori* come in? By way of
contrast, might be Balthasar's best answer. By contrast with the
religious *a priori*, the theological *a priori*, while taking the
religious *a priori* for granted, differs from it in being distinctively Christological and Trinitarian in character. It is what
enables our response to the new light of Christ granting human
beings as this does a participation in the uncreated light of the
Holy Trinity. The theological *a priori* is the 'transcendental'
presupposition of our sharing in the inner life of the Trinity
through Jesus Christ on the basis of a connaturality with the
divine Persons given by the Mediator, the God-man, when he
took what was ours (namely, humanity), so as to give us a share
in what is his (namely, divinity). Amazingly, it becomes second
nature to us (hence, 'connaturality') to be, through Christ, in
tune with the triune God.

In sum: the religious *a priori* enables us to perceive the
objective light of the Creator in the forms of the creation,
whereas the theological *a priori* enables us to perceive the
objective light of the Trinity in the historical form of Jesus
Christ. This second 'transcendental' structure is not inbuilt at
creation, it is a matter, rather, of God's 'second' gift, in a new
order of the divine generosity. Entirely gratuitous, it is a fresh
gift of a connaturality with the divine that goes beyond our
natural imagehood of God. It brings about what Balthasar terms
a new 'proportionality' between man and the divine Trinity –
something that can in no way be inferred from the nature of the
human spirit, not even in the dynamic orientation to God creation confers upon us. The theological *a priori* concerns itself
with the distinctively Christian experience *as irreducible to any
other*, no matter how religious.

The manner of expression shaped by the theological *a priori* may draw on genres known to 'religious man' at large – but what is done with them through the Gospel differs utterly. Myth is now actualised. In the bodily Resurrection of the incarnate humanity of the Word, the literal and particular are carried into the vertical transcendent realm in a final and eternal manner. The symbol takes root in the reality of ever-lasting being. The images used in biblical revelation may have affinities with those the mythopoeic imagination uses in this or that extra-biblical culture to express its sense of the Eternal. The shapes of human imagining are not, indeed, to be expunged. Rather, the forms of natural, man-generated, aesthetic, if they admit the Christ-form, will be given a transcendent relation to the supernatural. In his study *Science, Religion and Christianity,* Balthasar praises Baroque literature and art for having so imaginatively played out the realisation of the figures of Greek myth – Orpheus, Odysseus, Eros – in the person of the historic Christ.[57] As C. S. Lewis liked to remark, myth has become fact. Or, as Balthasar puts it, the truth of Jesus Christ is found at the point where what he calls, in the metaphysics volume of his Theo-aesthetics, the 'two piers' of myth and philosophy can finally be made to form an entire bridge. Myth tries to make sense of the world through concrete images. Philosophy tries to make sense of the world through articulating universal truth. They reach out towards each other, but never quite meet. The ineluctable growth of the philosophic impulse pushed myth toward the periphery of the human imagination. Myth continued to exist but without philosophy it became increasingly enclosed in gnostic fantasy. Philosophy then became cut off from doxology and prayer which had been instinctive for myth, and its concept of human reason narrowed. When the religious *a priori* gives way to the theological *a priori* these ills can be healed, this rupture in humanity's quest for a truth that would also be beauty repaired.

We have here one major source of Balthasar's disagreement with the approach of his erstwhile fellow Jesuit, Karl Rahner. To Balthasar's mind, Rahner made a great mistake in blocking

together the theological *a priori* with its merely religious counterpart. Rahner's vocabulary is partly the same and partly different, which could make comparison confusing. But the upshot is
that Rahner *tends* to treat the Trinitarian and Christological
revelation as simply the fullest (in Rahner's word) 'thematisa-
tion' or conscious, explicit articulation of a piety which is itself
not yet 'thematic' – not consciously, explicitly articulated – but,
at least in principle, pre-contains the content of the supreme
revelation since our intellectual nature is turned towards the
human-divine encounter, without our being aware of it, from the
very start. For Balthasar, this renders the given, historic revelation vulnerable to what some would frankly call 'demythologising' and others, more politely, 'resolution into its transcendental
formality'. It seems to come down to much the same thing. (This
is the argument of Balthasar's little polemical work *Cordula*,
translated into English as *The Moment of Christian Witness*[58].)
What Balthasar objects to in Rahner's theology of faith is that it
fails to derive faith from the *form* of Christ. Christ's form does
not verify itself (as it should) by virtue of the unique evidence
contained in its amazing and unexpected beauty. Instead, it
commends itself by its ability to satisfy, especially on the level
of the understanding, a drive towards transcendence already
entirely operative in peoples' lives (so no great surprise is
involved). Balthasar sees Rahner as, so to speak, almost half way
down the road to Rudolph Bultmann, for whom God cannot be
known objectively in the image of Christ but only non-
objectively as the condition of possibility for the human self-
understanding that occurs on the occasion of hearing the Gospel
of Christ.[59]

Balthasar shows his forthright commitment to the Christian
revelation in its irreducibly specific pattern when he insists that,
in collaboration with this inner grace, the form of Christ makes
for a new revelation with its own evidence which no insight into
the dynamism of the human spirit in its tendency towards God
can either anticipate in advance or verify in retrospect. There is
in fact no *need* at all in man that can explain or authenticate the

words and deeds of Christ. Only Christ's form makes those words and deeds lucidly plain. The '*a posteriori*', historical, evidence of that form is what founds Christian faith, not some '*a priori*', ahistorical state of affairs which has come into consciousness for this or that individual through prompting by the general *a posteriori* experience. In any case, what human expectation could envisage a triune, totally self-sufficient Creator becoming man in a tiny speck of dust somewhere in the universe and presenting his own extremity of humiliation, suffering – both physical and spiritual – and substitutionary death as the very form of life for all mankind? This rhetorical question identifies Balthasar's most basic theological conviction. Nowhere else but in the historical form of Jesus could anyone find the evidence to verify so extravagantly wasteful a love on the side of divinity and so utterly devastating a burden on the side of humanity. As Balthasar puts it in his theology of the Easter Triduum, no human evolution, hope or desire can unite the Hellish destruction of Good Friday with the splendid affirmation of Easter Sunday.[60] Only Jesus' form can verify a triune God who knows no need to subject himself to such horrors and yet in his total freedom does so. The evidence of the form of Christ is thus akin, Balthasar argues, to that of an artistic masterpiece. This form knows no external necessity in either divine or human reality, yet once we apprehend it we see that it 'must' be as it is.

Balthasar stresses the rupture and transformation that Christian conversion entails. *Pace* Rahner, it is not simply a matter of one who is already an anonymous Christian becoming so openly by name. For the Old Testament, as the Book of Exodus testifies, human beings were told by God, 'Man shall not see me and live'[61]. The New Testament fulfils this. We died to ourselves in God when we were converted to Christ and then we were brought to life again. In Jesus, the believer *has* for the first time *seen* God. It follows that what is incomprehensible in God no longer proceeds from mere ignorance. Rather is it the daunting, stupefying incomprehensibility of the fact that God so loved the world as to give his only Son. The God of all plenitude lowered himself not only by entering his creation as a creature but by entering it in the conditions of an existence determined by sin, destined for death, removed from God. Such was his amazing grace.

The relation of apologetics to dogmatics

One important corollary of Balthasar's estimate of the respective roles of the subjective and objective evidence for Christian revelation is a shift – for those inclined to accept his approach – in the relation of apologetics to dogmatic theology. These are two of the most important branches of Christian thought, so this is no bagatelle. Through his theological aesthetics, Balthasar seeks to modify the currently understood picture of apologetics by presenting apologetics as incipient dogmatics. For Balthasar, investigating the motives of credibility – the ways in which revelation commends itself to us on the ordinary rational level – is constantly on the point of trembling into loving prostration before the figure of the Word incarnate.

Here a bit of background may be useful. There were Christian apologists from the first generations of the Church after the apostles. But the first Catholic theologian to treat the issue of apologetics in a fully systematic fashion is usually reckoned to be the thirteenth-century German Dominican St Albert the Great. His 'antecedents of the act of faith', *antecedentia fidei*, include the most important theses of what we now call fundamental theology. They concern especially the metaphysical presuppositions of divine revelation, the fact of such divine revelation in Christ, and the character of Scripture as the witness to that revelation.[62] One question Albert did not settle clearly was the relation of these 'antecedents' to the certainty aspect of faith. The problem of the kind of certainty produced by apologetic argumentation and its relation to the free and supernatural character of the act of faith was one that long troubled the Schoolmen. Some masters of the early High Scholastic period –

such as William of Auxerre, William of Auvergne, and Philip the Chancellor – admitted two sorts of faith. The motives of credibility were said to produce 'intellectual faith' (other terms were also in use), which, said these thinkers, should be distinguished from faith in the full theological sense of the word. Merely intellectual faith, precisely because it rested on the rational force of arguments, had neither the religious nor the moral value of the virtue of theological faith – properly Christian faith – in the strict sense. That virtue is virtuous precisely because it has the character of an unconditional response to God as the 'First Truth', *Prima Veritas*, made possible by sharing in a more than natural light – by sharing a light, in fact, that is the light of supernatural faith proper, called by the Scholastics the *lumen fidei*. It is noteworthy that both Albert and Thomas are disinclined to give what the cathedral masters called 'intellectual faith' or some synonym thereof the title of 'faith' at all. The motives of credibility – such considerations as the Saviour's miracles and his fulfilment of prophecy, the sublimity of his teaching and his ethical perfection – may make people certain in *some* kind of adhering to the bearer of revelation (such adhering was sometimes known as *certitudo adhaesionis*, 'certainty of adhesion'). But this is not as yet the recognition of Jesus Christ as the very Word of the Father.

Over against, in particular, early Deist thinkers, Catholic writers from the sixteenth century onwards stressed the importance of the rational motives of credibility. Though in the later part of that century, owing to the challenge of Protestantism, a section 'on the Church', *de Ecclesia*, was customarily added to Catholic treatises on apologetics, the main content of Catholic apologetics for divine revelation did not differ greatly from that treated by their Protestant counterparts. The classic Catholic representatives of this stream undertook to prove the principles of both natural and revealed religion, moving through an account of natural theology and natural law to treatment of the possibility, utility and necessity of supernatural revelation, and the features of miracle and fulfilled prophecy which (especially) enable one to recognise a divine mission in act, the whole thing ending up with a discussion of the claims of the Church and the principles of Catholic faith. From the mid-eighteenth century on, this structure remains largely constant up until the manuals in use in the 1920s and beyond.[63] This was so even if in another way these treatises were always being modified, pouring into the seventeenth- and eighteenth-century mould discussions with such thinkers as Kant, Hegel, Schelling, Darwin, the history-of-religions school of empirical scholarship, Liberal Protestantism and Modernism. But by the time Balthasar was setting out to begin his lifelong study of Christian thought, in the 1920s and 1930s, some Catholic philosophers and theologians were declaring a degree of dissatisfaction with the entire approach.

Why might that be? The main criticism, and one Balthasar largely shared, was that such treatises claimed to establish the *fact* of divine revelation without ever envisaging the *meaning* of its content. Painting with broad brush-strokes: in these works the relation of supernatural truth to human realities was not manifest. And while that relation wholly exceeds what human beings could ever expect, so Balthasar would want to add, the wonderful character of that excess was not brought home. Presumably the Gospel offers an intelligible message – something we are meant to understand, even if this 'something', by its grandeur, also stretches our powers to a point where only the gracious enhancement of our capacities can serve our turn. (Where the appropriate paradigm of knowledge is love, then understanding and mystery will develop together, in direct proportion to each other.) But such was the emphasis on the proof of revelation by arguments external to itself that this intelligibility (even if it were an intelligibility with a depth of mystery to it) failed to make a proper appearance in justifying revelation's claims. Hence the critical epithet 'extrinsicist' applied to these schemes: the supernatural order seemed to be externally added on to the natural as an autonomous supplement, rather than fully integrated with the natural and suitably interiorised there.

Where Catholic apologetics was concerned, the single most influential dissentient voice was the French philosopher and lay theologian Maurice Blondel.[64] Without disputing that *some* place should be given to the considerations adduced in early modern apologetics, Blondel proposed to give the lion's share, in any commendation of revealed religion, to an account of how the internal logic of the act of faith corresponds to the 'logic' of the highest kind of human activity we know: namely, when we set out to discern *meaning* – and (especially) the *fullness of meaning* – in human life at large. It is not enough to adduce arguments to show the fact of divine attestation to Jesus. The mystery of Christ must be presented as throwing light on the whole human condition. The question is not so much to prove by miraculous facts the rights of Jesus as divine legate (though this is certainly not illegitimate, and can even be called necessary), but, in Balthasarian terms, to discern in the 'figure' of Jesus, his acts and destiny, a divine-human presence penetrating and transforming our sense of relation with God, with the world, with other persons and indeed with ourselves. In so doing, the Revealer, so we discern, confers on human history the weight of eternity. Naturally enough, this cannot be done without treating the *content of revelation from within*, rather than simply the *fact of revelation from without*. What Balthasar is attempting in the theological aesthetics coheres with much of this Blondelian programme, though his manner of pursuing its agenda is entirely his own.[65] Certainly, Balthasar had no desire to replace an extrinsicist apologetics with an apologetics of natural immanence. As he wrote:

> *[T]he tradition never set the criterion for the truth of revelation in the centre of the pious human subject, it never measured the abyss of grace by the abyss of need or sin, it never judged the content of dogma according to its beneficial effects on human beings. The Spirit does not reveal himself; he reveals the*

> *Father in the Son, who has become man.*
> *And the Son never allows himself to become*
> *re-absorbed in the human spirit ...*[66]

How then does Balthasar proceed? His first step is to show that beauty is a possible vehicle for divine self-manifestation. As we have seen, considered ontologically, beauty is not just a property of all created things *qua* created. What appears in the beauty of created forms is the radiance of being, *der Glanz des Seins.* Beauty thus speaks of the meaning of that which transcends and yet inheres in all existents.

Secondly, Balthasar treats beauty as the vehicle of the actual revelation of God in Christ, a revelation made when the eternal manifests itself in a concrete, material form, breaking into this world, as beauty does, numinously (for beauty, in words Balthasar liked to quote from Rilke's *Duino Elegies,* is the beginning of the terrible[67]). In the case of revelation, this means the eternal breaking in with the glory that truly inheres in the form of Jesus Christ. The epiphany of this form is not just sheerly overwhelming, however, for exploration of the career and fate of Jesus shows it is an intelligible history. This form is a narrative form, and the meaning of the story is divine love. Here the content and the form are one since both are wonderful. The content is as marvellously beautiful as is the form, and Balthasar's explanation for this is that both content and form reflect *love.* Love shares the structure of beauty. It confronts us with the mystery of the otherness of some other and calls forth a corresponding wonder and admiration.

Thirdly and finally, Balthasar develops his theological aesthetics in two parts that are, however, strongly unified as well as distinct. And this two-in-one exposition spans the separate treatises of (early modern and modern) apologetics and dogmatics. This is so because Balthasar's aesthetics is not only an epistemological investigation of the kind of 'seeing' involved in faith. It is also a doctrine of what he terms 'ecstasy'. There is 'ecstasy', first, in the going out (in Greek, *ek-stasis*) of the Godhead in weakness into the world as the manifestation of the love that is interior to the divine glory. There is 'ecstasy', secondly, in the way the believer is seized by the divine glory in this revelation in Jesus Christ and is taken up thereby into a share in the life of God himself. Ecstasy, so understood, contains in principle all the main themes of dogmatics – the Trinity, Christology, the doctrines of justification and sanctification, as well as of the sacraments, the Church and eschatology, the Last Things. Faith is a response to the radiance of what St Thomas calls the *bonum repromissum*, the beautifully ordered whole of salvation that is offered to us, exceeding any such 'whole' that exists *within* the world.[68]

So what we have here is a tendency to elide, without however ever completely denying, the distinction between apologetics and dogmatics just because Balthasar wants to elide, without however ever completely denying, the distinction between what the Schoolmen called 'certainty of adhesion' and the virtue of theological faith properly so called – the faith that, corresponded to in loving conversion, justifies and saves.

Balthasar can proceed in this direction because he doesn't think that what explains the act of faith is *simply* rationally available materials plus an elevation of human judgment by supernatural light. In his view, there is not only God's gracious supplying of more light with which to judge materials accessible to any reasonable person supplied with appropriate historical data about Jesus and arguments to back up those data. There is also, he maintains, a 'light' that shines forth from those materials themselves in their beautiful ordering in Jesus' person, life and work. The act of faith needs both kinds of light: light from within – where God can affect my powers of knowing and willing internally, since as my Creator he is closer to me than I am to myself, and light from without – light striking one from Jesus Christ himself as a figure in history who is made palpable to me in the preaching and Liturgy of the Church. On the one hand, the glory of the divine self-emptying in Jesus Christ can be seen only by 'eyes of faith' when God has prepared me interiorly to be receptive to Christ. On the other hand, the 'eyes of faith' can only see when the light of faith falls on them from the divine form that Jesus is. What the eyes of faith see when this interplay of light works as it should is the opening of the divine heart in love, the self-disclosure of the Trinity.

Conclusion on aesthetics

It is in the lives of saints and mystics that the inspired seeing which animates the Christian life in general and theological aesthetics in particular is most fully in act. Balthasar identifies its key as *humility*, which is the readiness to accept the gift of the divine love as it is, to appreciate the necessary and rightness of the form of the divine revelation as we are given it. Much of Balthasar's celebrated concern with the practice of holiness as a precondition of fruitful theologising belongs here; adoration and obedience follow from humility, and draw good theology in their train.[69] Henri de Lubac once contrasted Balthasar's theology with Hegel's. Whereas Hegel called his own thought a 'speculative Good Friday', de Lubac calls Balthasar's a 'contemplative Holy Saturday'. Evidently, I note in passing, de Lubac was not 'phased' by Balthasar's theology of the Descent into Hell which turns, of course, on the events of the first Holy Saturday: perhaps he realised that for Balthasar while the Descent is, unlike for most of Catholic tradition, the end-point of the mysteries of Christ's humiliation, it is also, in keeping with Catholic tradition, the starting-point of the mysteries of his exaltation.[70] The useful phrase 'contemplative Holy Saturday', in the wider meaning de Lubac intended for it, brings out the degree to which Balthasar's material dogmatics are informed by his fundamental theological insight into the nature of faith as contemplative seeing, as well as the extent to which his theology centres on the self-emptying of the Son of God which reaches full term in the Descent into Hell.

It also reminds us that the final volumes of the theological aesthetics consist in a reading of the Old and New Testament.[71]

Balthasar at the close of this massive work turns again to the Bible in the hope that, now we grasp what is at stake in theological aesthetics, we can read the Scriptures with new eyes. If we do so, we shall see how though the New Testament's amazing consummation of the Old, the mystery of all creation, man included, received its definitive interpretation as the hidden presence of Absolute Love, to which, in its luminous, bountiful and exuberant character, beauty's qualities of clarity, integrity and proportion, by analogy, belong. See too how the recipients of God's self-revelation – ourselves – receive thereby the call to make the divine visible in charity, the specifically Christian love of God and neighbour, the intended moral outcome of Balthasar's entire work. These statements are not only conclusions drawn from his theological aesthetics. They are also anticipations of the message of his theological dramatics and theological logic as well.

[22] 'Revelation and the Beautiful', art. cit., p. 96.
[23] *The Glory of the Lord. A Theological Aesthetic I. Seeing the Form*, op. cit., pp. 18–19.
[24] 'Revelation and the Beautiful', art. cit., p. 110.
[25] Ibid., p. 109. This is the upshot of the lengthy exploration of the history of metaphysics in *The Glory of the Lord. A Theological Aesthetics IV. The Realm of Metaphysics in Antiquity* (San Francisco, Ignatius, 1989); *The Glory of the Lord. A Theological Aesthetics V. The Realm of Metaphysics in the Modern Age* (San Francisco, Ignatius, 1991).
[26] 1 John 1–3.
[27] G. K. Chesterton, *St Thomas Aquinas* (London, Sheed and Ward, 1933), pp. 138–139. Incidentally, Balthasar held a high opinion of Chesterton. In a passage relevant to the present topic – the positive valuation of sensuousness, Balthasar wrote, 'Chesterton is right that the world is full of Christian ideas gone mad': *Man in History* (London and Sydney, Geoffrey Chapman, 1967), pp. 174–175. Actually, Chesterton had written (in *Orthodoxy*) not so much of Christian ideas dispersed with anarchic effect into the world but Christian *virtues*.
[28] See H. Pouillon, 'La Beauté, propriété transcendentale chez les scolastiques (1220–1290)', *Archives d'histoire doctrinale et littéraire au moyen âge* 15 (1946), pp. 263–328.
[29] J. Maritain, *Art et Scolastique* (Paris, Louis Rouart et Fils, 1927, 2nd edition), p. 74.
[30] More widely, it stands at the point of confluence of a number of streams of thought – Platonic, Aristotelean, neo-Platonist, Goethean, Thomistic, as well

as issuing from the work of the Austrian psychologist and philosopher Christian von Ehrenfels who coined the phrase 'Gestalt psychology'. See D. C. Schindler, 'Reason in Mystery. Gestalt: Knowledge and Aesthetic Experience in Balthasar and Augustine', *Second Spring* 6 (2004), pp. 23–33 and here at pp. 26–28.

[31] G. K. Chesterton, *St Thomas Aquinas*, op. cit., pp. 188–189.

[32] H. A. Hodges, reviewing *Herrlichkeit I* and *II* in the *Journal of Theological Studies* N. S. 17 (1966), pp. 524–538, and here at p. 528.

[33] One of the lessons Balthasar's aesthetics would convey is that what is valuable in Romanticism needs to be established on a new ground – the ground of the perennial philosophy, tutored by revelation: see *The Glory of the Lord. A Theological Aesthetic I. Seeing the Form*, op. cit., p. 104.

[34] S. van Erp, *The Art of Theology*, op. cit., p. 133.

[35] 'Revelation and the Beautiful', art. cit., p. 118.

[36] Ibid., p. 116.

[37] *The Glory of the Lord. A Theological Aesthetic IV. The Realm of Metaphysics in Antiquity*, op. cit., pp. 23–25.

[38] *Mysterium Paschale. The Mystery of Easter* (Edinburgh, T. & T. Clark, 1990), pp. 11–48.

[39] 'Revelation and the Beautiful', art. cit., p. 113.

[40] Ibid., pp. 113–114. On the importance of the category of 'uniqueness' in Balthasar's thinking, see J. Disse, *Metaphysik der Singularität. Eine Hinführung am Leitfaden der Philosophie Hans Urs von Balthasars* (Vienna, Passagen, 1996).

[41] 'Revelation and the Beautiful', art. cit., p. 105.

[42] 'I will argue that the self is unified when it is guided by aesthetic form', thus F. A. Murphy, *Christ the Form of Beauty. A Study in Theology and Literature* (Edinburgh, T. & T. Clark, 1995), p. 13.

[43] Ibid., p. 184, where the author writes, in connexion with Balthasar and moving towards the conclusion of her study: 'The form of Christ turns outwardness toward human intuition. He turns human inwardness toward transcendent reality by giving it a pattern of action to repeat, or a shape to the imagination'.

[44] For a recent recovery of a high doctrine of the imagination, indebted to Coleridge, see D. Hedley, *Living Forms of the Imagination* (Edinburgh, T. & T. Clark, 2008).

[45] R. A. Johnson, *The Origins of Demythologizing: Philosophy and Historiography in the Theology of Rudolph Bultmann* (Leiden, Brill, 1974).

[46] Thomas Aquinas, *Summa theologiae*, Ia., q. 39, a. 8.

[47] I have attempted my own version of this approach: see A. Nichols, O. P., *The Art of God Incarnate. Theology and Image in Christian Tradition* (London, Darton, Longman and Todd, 1980).

[48] *The Glory of the Lord. A Theological Aesthetics IV. The Realm of Metaphysics in Antiquity*, op. cit., p. 14.

[49] This is Balthasar's 'meta-anthropology': a not very transparent term but one he chose himself, and well-explained in R. A. Howsare, *Balthasar. A Guide*

for the Perplexed (London and New York, T. & T. Clark, 2009), pp. 50–53. Howsare's book is a superb overall introduction to Balthasar and his work.

[50]   S. van Erp, *The Art of Theology*, op. cit., p. 138.

[51]   Cf. Thomas Aquinas, *Summa theologiae* IIa. IIae., q. 4, a. 1: 'Faith is that habit of mind whereby eternal life begins in us'.

[52]   G. K. Chesterton, *St Thomas Aquinas*, op. cit., p. 221.

[53]   In Bultmann's *Jesus Christ and Mythology* (New York, Scribner, 1958), the German scholar makes it plain that for him the facts on which faith rests are not lodged in the empirical world. It is only in 'mythological thinking' that 'the action of God, whether in nature, history, human fortune or the inner life of the soul is understood as an action which intervenes within the natural or historical or psychological course of events', ibid., p. 61.

[54]   *The Glory of the Lord. A Theological Aesthetics II. Studies in Theological Style: Clerical Styles* (San Francisco, Ignatius, 1984); *The Glory of the Lord. A Theological Aesthetics III. Studies in Theological Style: Lay Styles* (San Francisco, Ignatius, 1986).

[55]   *The Glory of the Lord. A Theological Aesthetics III. Studies in Theological Style: Lay Styles*, op. cit., pp. 105–171.

[56]   R. Viladesau, *Beauty of the Cross. The Passion of Christ in Theology and the Arts, from the Catacombs to the Eve of the Renaissance* (New York and Oxford, Oxford University Press, 2006).

[57]   *Science, Religion and Christianity* (London, Burns and Oates, 1958), p. 64.

[58]   *The Moment of Christian Witness* (New York, Newman Press, 1968). Rahner's position is, however, more subtle than that of some Rahnerians: see A. Nichols, O. P., 'Rahner and Balthasar: The Anonymous Christianity Debate Revisited', in idem., *Beyond the Blue Glass. Catholic Essays on Faith and Culture I* (London, Saint Austin Press, 2002), pp. 107–128.

[59]   A somewhat similar position to Rahner's is occupied by his fellow Jesuit the Canadian Bernard Lonergan, for whom all images with their sensuous, *a posteriori* evidence are objectifications of the transcendental notions by which the human spirit expresses itself in its longing for the Absolute, God, and the graced fulfilment of that longing. Always precarious, such images are ultimately to lose their relevance and disappear. Lonergan's wider scheme, which somewhat devalues both images and concepts as the 'outer word' (merely) of revelation, is described in A. Nichols, O. P., 'Lonergan's *Method in Theology* and the Theory of Paradigms', in idem., *Scribe of the Kingdom. Essays on Theology and Culture II* (London, Sheed and Ward, 1994), pp. 54–75, and especially pp. 60–63.

[60]   *Mysterium Paschale. The Mystery of Easter*, op. cit., pp. 49–88.

[61]   Exodus 33:20.

[62]   There is a magisterial study of these matters in German: A. Lang, *Die Entwicklung des apologetischen Problems in der Scholastik des Mittelalters* (Freiburg, Herder, 1962).

[63]   See, for example, A. Tanquerey, *Synopsis theologicae dogmaticae fundamentalis* (Paris, Desclée, 1927, 22nd edition); C. Pesch, *Compendium theologiae dogmaticae*, I (Freiburg, Herder, 1926, 3rd edition).

48   A KEY TO BALTHASAR

[64] An English translation of two highly pertinent essays is found in M. Blondel, *The Letter on Apologetics and History and Dogma* ([1964] Grand Rapids, Eerdmans, 1994), with an introductory essay by Alexander Dru and Dom Illtyd Trethowan which usefully outlines the thinking contained in Blondel's masterpiece *L'Action*, the key to his work.

[65] I note Balthasar's acuter (and to some extent, countervailing) emphasis on the – 'splendid' – objectivity of the phenomenon of Christ, surpassing all that natural need could suggest, in A. Nichols, O. P., *From Hermes to Benedict XVI. Faith and Reason in Modern Catholic Thought* (Leominster, Gracewing, 2009), pp. 192–196, though Balthasar's criticisms were directed not so much at Blondel as at Rousselot who might be deemed, in this aspect of his writing, a Blondelian *à l'outrance*. I have already had occasion to mention this figure (but as a student of St Thomas) in Chapter One, note 3.

[66] *Love Alone is Credible* (San Francisco, Ignatius, 2005), p. 43.

[67] 'Revelation and the Beautiful', art. cit., p. 106; *The Glory of the Lord. A Theological Aesthetics I. Seeing the Form,* op. cit., p. 390.

[68] In his commentary on Chapter 11 of the Letter to the Hebrews Thomas explains how the Writer can describe faith in terms of hope: the goal of faith is no different from its object, because it is the 'vision of God which comprises the other goods we desire to attain': see L. J. Elders, *Sur les traces de saint Thomas d'Aquin théologien. Etude de ses commentaries bibliques. Thèmes théologiques* (Paris, Parole et Silence, 2009), p. 211.

[69] 'Theology and Holiness', *Communio* 16 (1987), pp. 483–490. The earliest version of this essay dates back as far as 1948. Re-written in different contexts, its role in Balthasar's work is well-treated in the memorial issue of the French edition of *Communio* produced on Balthasar's death: G. Chantraine, 'Théologie et sainteté', *Communio* XIV (1989), pp. 54–81.

[70] I refer here to the controversy aroused by A. L. Pitstick, *Light in Darkness: Hans Urs von Balthasar and the Catholic Doctrine of Christ's Descent into Hell* (Grand Rapids, Eerdmans, 2007). Though there are difficulties, perhaps insuperable ones, in the imagistic thinking Balthasar brings into play when speaking about the experience of Christ in the world of the dead, it does not seem impossible to suppose that a mystery with a kenotic beginning cannot have a glorious conclusion. The way to reconcile (some version of) Balthasar's theologoumenon about the Descent as a negative hiatus with the conviction of the Tradition that it is the initiation of the Easter triumph would seem to lie along these lines.

[71] *The Glory of the Lord. A Theological Aesthetics VI. Theology: the Old Covenant* (San Francisco, Ignatius, 1991); *The Glory of the Lord. A Theological Aesthetics VII. Theology: the New Covenant* (San Francisco, Ignatius, 1989).

Chapter Three

Key-word 'Freedom':

Balthasar on the Good

Introduction

Having looked at God's saving mystery in our regard from the perspective of form, which corresponds to the analogate of beauty, we must now look at that mystery in the perspective of its self-realisation, which corresponds to the analogate of the good. The beauty of Christ is not that of an icon, simply, or a luminous form crystallised in immobile perfection. It is the beauty of a dramatic action, which opens the revolving movement in the Trinity to human apprehension and shows it to be *philanthropically active* in our regard – that is, concerned to intervene for our good. Then from there we shall have to go on (in Chapter Three) to consider it in the perspective of its logic, which corresponds to the analogate of truth. But meanwhile (in the present chapter) we need to concentrate on how the self-realisation of God's saving mystery is in fact the realisation of the supreme good for man, and how it unfolds in a transforming encounter between two freedoms – infinite, uncreated freedom and finite created freedom, doing so in a drama where the players are not only human but divine.

As its name implies, Balthasar's *Theodramatik* is a 'theological dramatics': a way of understanding divine revelation on the basis of the theatre, of drama. Balthasar thinks it plain that what we are presented with in revelation is not simply ideas, or attitudes, or even narratives. Rather, in and through ideas, attitudes, and narratives, we are presented with an *action* – an action that is at once complex and unitary, with agents both divine and human. It is, as will appear, a wondrously philanthropic action, concerned with divine initiative to achieve the good for man. No account of salvation can avoid all suggestion of drama enacted.

The drama of salvation

If then we turn to consider what the theatre is – what drama is – we soon surmise that drama could provide an excellent model for the saving revelation. In drama, actors interact so that in playing their roles in relation to each other, we the audience gain a disclosure of what human life is like (we may think we know already, but how much human life is *unexamined* life!), and in so doing become ourselves somehow changed. We are, or we feel we are, purified and enlarged in our vision as we stumble out of the theatre into the ordinary world. We seem transformed, somehow different, at least for a while – and perhaps longer.

In Balthasar's analysis of the drama, which occupies (along with examples of significant theatre) much of the opening volume of *Theo-drama*[72] , there are six factors, arranged by him in two sets of three. First, there is a trio concerned with the production of the play. That trio consists of the author, the actor (or actors) and the director. Then there is the trio involved in the realisation of the drama: summed up by Balthasar as the performance, the public and what he terms the 'horizon' of the play. By the latter he means the perspective on human existence which the drama opens up for those who assist with attention at its unfolding and are drawn into its course, in some way participating in what happens.

Applying this to the divine revelation enacted for our salvation, what do we find? The author of the 'theo-drama' is of course the Father from whom, as Balthasar puts it, everything proceeds. The author – the Father – is responsible for all. The Father is before the play and above it, yet through his own dramatic script, his *Dichtung*, he is included or incorporated in the play in the strongest and most irrevocable sense. He does not, however, actually perform the piece. For this we need an actor, who, as Balthasar says, bestows on the words of the author their real presence as action. With the help of ideas from philosophers and others who have studied the concept of drama, Balthasar points out that the actor – and in theo-drama the chief actor is the divine Son made man – is not simply a servant of the script, the author's text. Though deeply one with it, he is also in a certain way free in its regard. The actor situates his acting in a tension between sympathy for the author's writing and mastery over it. Or better, he overcomes that antithesis by a perfect readiness or well-disposedness, *Verfügbarkeit* (the French have a good word for it, *disponibilité*), to follow where both the author's intention and his own inspired reading of the significance of the text are leading.

There is, though, a third necessary figure in the production of the drama, and that is the director, the *Regisseur*, whom in English we call indeed the 'producer'. In theo-drama, the producer is the Holy Spirit. What is his task? A director's task is to transpose the playwright's text into the reality of the performance, in the light of the various contingent needs or emergencies that may arise even in the best-kept theatre, and in relation to the fluctuating capacities of the repertory company as a whole: some of whom may be having breakdowns, throwing tantrums or simply losing their voice. The producer's job is to be faithfully obedient to the text but yet to recreate it as a unity in and through the varied company that is his troupe of players. By his own imagination, the director thus performs an essential service to both author and company of actors.

The first trio – author, principal actor, producer – are, then, Father, Son and Holy Spirit: the Trinity at once in itself and in its relations with the world. The Father's script concerns, we can say, self-emptying: it expresses renunciation, humility, compassion, sacrificial love. The Son acts out the role of the self-emptier with which he is completely identified. He does so by a combination of faithful translation and creative inspiration, by the concurrence of the two wills, divine and human, as these are united in his single theandric (divine-human) person. The Holy

Spirit guides the Son in his performance, not least in enabling him to interact appropriately with the other characters in the play.

So much for the first trio. That leaves the second: the performance itself, the public and the horizon. It is by means of this second trio that the Trinity draws us into the dramatic action in the theatre of the world. For in this production, the spectators do not simply participate in the action by empathy as they watch it unfold. In this play, the mode of production is rather *avant-garde*. People pass from the auditorium onto the stage. Indeed, as Balthasar puts it, in the last analysis there is no one who can remain a pure spectator. All have some part to play. As for the horizon, the perspective which the play opens up, this is nothing other than the comprehensive event of the Trinitarian self-communication as the engracing of the world.

The message of theo-drama

For Balthasar perhaps the single most important thing about theo-drama – its single most important message – is that in this play the Father no longer sits simply as judge of the *Weltspiel*, the drama of life, the play of the world as otherwise written, for good or evil, by the creativity of human beings in the setting of nature. He has his own script and in it he bends down to the sinful and suffering creature in the concrete form of his Son and his Spirit in order thereby to scoop us up and bring us to himself. The self-giving qualities of the human Jesus as led by the Holy Spirit do not simply manifest the self-emptying of the Logos in the Incarnation, accompanied and undergirded by the Holy Spirit. They also express the stooping down of the Father himself in the service of our redemption and consummation.[73] The Father's script is his own self-donation, and can only be so since the divine nature he possesses and the divine communion of life he both originates and shares with Son and Spirit are nothing other than sacrificial – kenotic – love.

But how can the immutable God enter the world-play in a fresh guise as love – and *kenotic* love, of all things, at that?

Balthasar offered his principal, if also highly succinct, explanation for that in the preface to the second edition of his *Mysterium Paschale*: his theology of the Paschal Mystery. In the intrinsic eternal constitution of the Trinitarian relations – relations that at once make these persons distinct from each other and yet place them in communion with each other, there is given the possibility of new modes in which Father, Son and Spirit can relate to each other via their activity in the creation which the Father, co-working with his Word and his Spirit, established in time, with time, and as time.[74] The aim of the fresh display of inner-Trinitarian kenotic love in the extra-Trinitarian economy of salvation will be the homecoming of redeemed man to God through enfolding in the communion of the Triune life.

The two freedoms

In the perspective of theo-drama, to say that the main agents in the work of salvation are at once divine and human is to speak of the inter-relation of two *freedoms*, one infinite and other finite. How can God and man act vis-à-vis one another without either the former – God – absorbing the latter – man – into his own infinitude, or the latter finitising the former, reducing God to a fellow-being? This question made it imperative for Balthasar to address the issue of the interplay of divine and human freedom head-on.

He found such an interplay to be feasible in two senses. First, such human-divine interplay is possible in the context of considering freedom as *autonomous motion* – freedom of choice, freedom of the will, what St Thomas had called *voluntas ut voluntas*, the will *as* will, as sheer capacity to opt for this or that kind of action in pursuit of our goals. Taking freedom to be of such a sort, we can say that human finitude, in exploring its possibilities, discovers its own ability to be the perpetrator of evil. Divorced from the counsel of God – from the divine plan – it may very well miss the road to its own fulfilment, not to say career off the road altogether and crash in smithereens. But God can use failure and tragedy, consequences of our 'autonomous motion', to recall us to himself. That is one helpful way to think about how human freedom relates itself to divine freedom. By and large, it is the approach of the second century Church Father St Irenaeus and the Greek patristic tradition generally.

But there is also a second way. And that is when freedom is considered rather more deeply as *our fundamental self-expression* as beings who are made for the good. This is what St Thomas calls *voluntas ut natura*, will as a way of speaking of our basic nature in its most fundamental, if often flawed and inefficacious, drive. In the context of this way of looking at will, we can say with the humanists of antiquity (and the Renaissance) that our nature demands from us a practical affirmation of the 'whole' – the universal good – over the 'part' we ourselves individually are. Spelling that out, it requires from us an affirmation of the transcendent Goodness, God, who is the good of the entire universe, the one whose likeness is spread abroad in all things. But for this affirmation really to be made by us, effectively, in practice – for us, by our behaviour, consistently to yield second place to the greater good of the whole, God's gracious Spirit must liberate our will from within. This is the only way whereby we can actually carry out what our nature prompts us, impotently, to perform. And this happens when finite freedom is allowed to share in the specifically divine quality of infinite freedom through the indwelling Holy Spirit. Balthasar calls this man's freedom to consent to God. It is the distinctive approach of St Augustine and the Latin patristic tradition generally.

From this account of the two ways in which we can think of finite freedom and infinite freedom inter-relating, inter-meshing, Balthasar moves on to the manner in which, in saving history, God has made of the relation between finite freedom and infinite freedom an unbreakable union. He moves on, in other words, to the place of the Mediator. On each scheme – and the schemes are not alternatives, for each of the two gives us a good slice of truth – the role of the Mediator is all-important.

First, on the Irenaean or 'Greek' scheme: the waywardness of the freedom of autonomous motion, as we know it in our sinful state, implies a rupture – some kind of conflictual distance – between God and man. This leads Balthasar to speak of the necessity of Jesus Christ as protagonist in the drama. Balthasar describes him in this perspective as one who is indispensable yet, to worldly prediction, incalculable; as the God-man who is the epitome of the drama in his own person; as torn asunder by the tragic divide to which his sharing of fallen humanity and all-holy divinity commits him, and yet, even as he is torn, healing the division. In a neatly turned remark of the distinguished American exegete Ben F. Meyer: 'In the light of the affirmation of God, the fact of evil cannot fail to become "the problem of evil"; but by the same token the problem cannot fail to have a solution'[75]. A redemptive Incarnation offering transformation through – and therefore *beyond* – tragedy is, evidently, the solution provided.

But then secondly, on the Augustinian or 'Latin' scheme: here Balthasar has a more subtle account to offer of the need, in the inter-relation of finite and infinite freedom, for the Word incarnate. There is a difficulty in showing how, in the consent of freedom, one who is infinite freedom can make space for a finite freedom to embrace him in a genuine consent – for these are not, by definition, two finite freedoms, meeting and greeting in a common space, on a level playing field. Balthasar believes we cannot do justice to the Latin doctrine of consensual freedom between man and God without bringing in to help us the theme of the eternal generation of the Word. We can only sort this one out because of what we learn – thanks to the entry onto the world stage of the Jesus who is the Trinitarian Son – from the eternal generation of the Word, in the mutual surrender of Father and Son, and the fruitfulness of that as shown in the spiration of the Holy Spirit.

What, then, *do* we see there? For Balthasar, we see how 'letting-be', making space for otherness, is the hallmark of freedom at its infinite divine pole. The negative distance between the world and God is grounded in a positive distance between God and his Logos, his eternal Word. The Father *can* relate to his own creatures as infinite freedom to a whole galaxy of centres of finite freedom, none of which loses its freedom through this relatedness to the Infinite but on the contrary salvages it, enhances it, thereby, rediscovering finite freedom in and through God himself. But this is only possible because of that primordial relationship whereby the Word responds to the generating Father by an obedience that is perfect coincidence with freedom. Here we have, if you like, a theo-dramatic version of the Pauline and Johannine doctrine of the coming to be of all creatures through the Word, a theo-dramatic rendering of it that applies that doctrine more specifically to *free* creatures able to participate actively as 'persons in the drama' in the theatre of the world.

Re-relating human freedom to divine freedom, all for the sake of human salvation, is the corresponding description of how Jesus Christ saves the world. It will take the Incarnation and – above all – the Cross to do it. As a French student of Balthasar's doctrine of salvation has explained:

> *[I]f the world, created in the Son and subsisting in*
> *him, can have no other 'locus' but within the*
> *difference of the hypostases [the Trinitarian*
> *persons], then the resounding of the creature's*
> *'No' can exist nowhere else but in this very*
> *same place (Stelle), within the absolute intra-*
> *divine difference; and when the Son becomes*
> *incarnate and penetrates into the darkness of*
> *the world, he is able to 'take the place' of*
> *darkness and 'substitute' (Stell-vertretung)*
> *himself for it by virtue of his very position*
> *in the Trinity.*[76]

And Antoine Birot goes on to emphasise (having in mind, no doubt, those who regard any doctrine of a *substitutionary* death as incompatible with the goodness of the Father) that it is human beings who impose this immeasurable burden on Jesus – though, to be sure, he is able to bear it and willing to accept it, thanks to the mission of redemption given him by the Father, a mission to which he consents in obedient joy. As the God-man who is on both sides of the Covenant between God and humanity simultaneously, he can re-present on the Cross not only the 'clash' between infinite and finite freedom but also – and here is the source of our joy – the reconciliation between them.[77] This is the heart of Balthasar's dramatic theology of our redemption – laid out with great power and comprehensiveness in *Theo-drama*'s fourth volume.[78]

Incidentally, it is the assent, given in our name by the Virgin Mary, at the foot of the Cross, to that primordial consent of the God-man, which for Balthasar grounds the subsequent participation of the redeemed in the saving act of the Redeemer – the participation that enables them to enjoy its fruits and submediate its power to others. So this is a good point to mention how Balthasar is a highly Marian theologian, meaning by that: a theologian who offers an exalted account of our Lady's significance, and not just one in whose writings she figures frequently.[79] Balthasar's high doctrine of the Mother of the Lord turns not only on his orthodox theology of the Incarnation (shared with all Church-recognised divines) but also on an audacious personal view of her role in the Atonement. At the Cross she becomes, according to Balthasar – in a Mariological interpretation seconded by Joseph Ratzinger, later Pope Benedict XVI – the 'primal Church', the depositary of all the saving good the Redeemer wills for his people.[80]

Why 'drama', not 'story'?

At a time when 'narrative theology' was making its appearance as a school of theological writing in Western Catholicism, it has sometimes been asked why Balthasar was so insistent that the transcendental good should be presented as a drama, and not a story. Why is it theo-drama and not theo-narration that interests him? One explanation runs: since sacred time breaks in on natural human living in an unaccountable way, it seems better to conceive of the relation between God and human beings in history in dramatic rather than narrative terms. In Francesca Aran Murphy's view:

> *Drama is open to breaks in the sequence,*
> *abrupt 'vertical' alterations of direction. The*
> *notion of story gives us a nice, rounded*
> *sense of an ending, of completion or closure.*
> *Stories and drama can be equally eventful,*
> *but nothing happens in a story which is not*
> *explained by something within the story.*
> *Whereas the events in drama hover on the*
> *edge of mystery, a story is entirely explicable*
> *on its own terms.*[81]

This is helpful, but more pertinent may be the praise of drama found in one of Balthasar's Germanist sources, Friedrich Wilhelm Joseph von Schelling, and notably the latter's (1802) work *The Philosophy of Art (Die Philosophie der Kunst)*.[82] For Schelling, drama is the genre that best advances the self-revelation of the Absolute. There seem to be two reasons for this conviction. Firstly, there is, in the words of the English priest-scholar David Potter:

> *the impression of immediacy [drama]*
> *creates by dispensing with both the*
> *subjective persona of lyric poetry and*
> *the retrospective narration of the epic.*[83]

But secondly, and more importantly, in Schelling's estimation comes:

> *the way in which drama synthesises*
> *the subjective freedom of lyrical self-*
> *analysis and the implacable*
> *necessity of the epic into an overall*
> *effect of complete objectivity.*[84]

In other words, drama is both more immediate and more comprehensively faithful to reality at large.

Moreover, Balthasar believed that all the main methodological elements in contemporary Christian theology were converging on the need for a dramatic theology, or rather a theological dramatic theory, which, however, would not be something essentially innovative but a matter of manifesting explicitly what has always been implied in the structure of revelation. As he writes in the first volume of the dramatics:

> *It is not a question of recasting theology*
> *into a new shape previously foreign to it.*
> *Theology itself must call for this shape; it*
> *must be something implicit within it,*
> *manifested explicitly too in many places.*
> *For theology could never be anything*
> *other than an explication of the revelation*
> *of the Old and New Covenants, their*
> *presuppositions (the created world) and*
> *purposes (its infusion with divine life).*
> *This revelation, however, in its total shape,*
> *in large-scale and in small-scale matters, is*
> *dramatic. It is the history of an initiative on*
> *God's part for his world, the history of a*
> *struggle between God and the creature over*
> *the latter's meaning and salvation.*[85]

We hear the continuing influence of Barth's predestination doctrine when Balthasar goes on to add that he will be careful not to pre-empt the question: Is the outcome of this struggle predetermined or uncertain (in various crucial respects)? Christ has expiated all the sins of the world, yet he will judge each human being according to his deserts. He has triumphed over the cosmic powers and won his final battle once for all, and yet those powers continue to dominate world history more than ever. Balthasar adds, therefore, a caveat:

> *Theology will always have to reflect on all*
> *this, without ever coming to a finished*

> *conclusion; however much it tries to create*
> *a systematic presentation, it must leave*
> *room for this dramatic aspect and find an*
> *appropriate form of thought for it.*[86]

That, of course, opens the issue, 'Dare we hope that all may be saved?' and it also indicates that Balthasar will not want, at any rate, to say we are straightforwardly certain that 'all can'.

From 'analogy of being' to 'analogy of freedom'

Christian theo-drama, so understood, will make its own the cycle of themes we have already touched on: the interplay of dramatic aspects in the revelation-event as an action involving God and man, divine and human freedom, rooted as this is in creation and prolonged to eschatology. This entails the self-involvement of God. As Balthasar writes:

> *Can we say that God has 'staked his all' on*
> *this play? What is meant by 'God's history',*
> *by his kenosis, by the death of the Son of*
> *God? What is the relation between the*
> *economic and the immanent Trinity in all*
> *this? And, since we cannot avoid those*
> *ultimate questions which form the core of*
> *theo-drama: Where is the path that leads*
> *between the two abysses of a systematics*
> *in which God, absolute Being, is only the*
> *Unmoved before whom the moving world*
> *plays out its drama, and a mythology*
> *which absorbs God into the world and makes*
> *him to be one of the warring parties of the*
> *world process?*[87]

The saving revelation is unthinkable if God is the uninvolved God of Deism – but the same is true if God is the 'absorbed' God of ancient Gnosticism and its modern equivalent, Hegelianism. Can theological dramatic theory avoid these dangers? Doubtless the jury is still out (perhaps not in heaven), but Balthasar thinks it can – through the idea, especially, of *analogia libertatis*, the 'analogy of freedom'.

One important thing that is happening in Balthasar's theological dramatics is that the theological doctrine or, if you prefer, the theological thesis of the analogy of being is undergoing a sea-change. To switch the metaphor from sailing to mechanical engineering, Balthasar is ratcheting it up to a higher level of operation. A theme running right through Balthasar's oeuvre is *the permutations of analogy.* In the theological dramatics, the 'analogy of being', that classic topic in a philosophical theology of creation, is made to serve an 'analogy of liberty', placed at the disposal of a dogmatic theology, and more specifically a theology of redemption. Ultimately, the 'analogy of liberty' (or 'of freedom') will turn into an 'analogy of charity', where the moral life and the mystical life – the key components of the life of holiness, and so the closest thing on earth to heaven – find their issue in the endless life of the Age to Come.

Christ as the concrete 'analogy of being'

Balthasar happily accepts the notion of the analogy of being, a commonplace of Catholic thought, notably in its Thomistic strain, but he soon finds he wants to give that notion, even in a discussion of creation, a nuance that comes from revelation and not just from natural wisdom *tout court*. He was encouraged in this by the discovery that, for the mediaeval Conciliar tradition, the scope of the analogy of being was not restricted to the natural realm.

Throughout his work, Balthasar makes repeated reference to the analogy between finite being and infinite Being. His earliest ideas on analogy come in fact from St Thomas, but it is a Thomas modulated by Erich Przywara – whom we encountered briefly in Chapter One. When Balthasar presents the common teaching of the Thomist school that God and the world are joined by an analogy of being on the basis of God's own creative production of the world in the God-world relationship, he emphasises, with the Fourth Lateran Council of 1215, how in all this there is always a 'greater dissimilarity', *maior dissimilitudo*, between God and the creature even at the heart of the participation of the creature in, and so its likeness to, the Being that comes from its Source. Increasingly, Balthasar interpreted Thomas' analogy of being in the light of the Thomist 'real distinction' between existence and essence. Only in God is his essence his existence. This is the true foundation of the 'greater dissimilarity'. 'Dissimilarity predominates', he wrote, for 'even the highest creature lacks the most divine attribute; it lacks self-subsistence'.[88]

Precisely because the analogy of being, so understood, is universally applicable, it was, he thought, a mistake to restrict it, as is usually done, to that relation between the infinite and the finite which is set up on the basis of God's creative act. The analogy of being is not just a way of speaking about natural being's participatory relation to the Being of its Source. On the contrary, the analogy of being is equally applicable to the rational creature's supernatural elevation by grace. The Fourth Lateran Council drew its key example of analogy-thinking from a comparison between the 'oneness' disciples enjoy in the 'union of charity in grace' and that 'oneness' which the divine persons enjoy 'in the sense of unity of identity in nature'. To identify analogy here picks up the cue of some weighty words of Jesus in his High Priestly Prayer, 'May they be one in as we also are one'[89].

So the principle of the analogy of being must also apply (here Balthasar draws the appropriate conclusion), to the 'highest union between divine and created being' and that is, for Christian revelation, the union found 'in the God-man himself'[90]. In other words, the *analogia entis* should be able to throw light on Jesus Christ as the Word incarnate through whom not only are all things made but likewise God is revealed, humanity saved and the world brought to its completion. Put at its most comprehensive, then: Balthasar looks at analogy operating not only in the God-world relationship originally established by the Creator, and its working out in the being of the God-man, but also how it functions in the relation between man and God which is necessary if divine revelation is to be comprehensible to man, and finally in the inter-relation of divine and human freedoms in salvation. In other words, the analogy of being is relevant not just to a theistic metaphysics, but also to Christology, to the theology of revelation and, finally, to a theology of redemption itself. In this, as we shall now see, analogy will move through its own permutations – from the analogy of being through the analogy of liberty, the analogy of freedom, to an analogy of love.

It was during his encounter with Barth that Balthasar learned how to give the analogy of being a Christological form – which sets this whole development in motion. Balthasar tried to win Barth's favour – not in any opportunistic sense – by re-contextualising the *analogia entis* within the *analogia fidei*, the 'analogy of faith': the inter-connexion of all aspects of revelation around their Christological centre. Barth had objected to the standard Catholic account that, surely, the relationship between creature and Creator is to be understood by reference not to being but to Jesus Christ. This relationship cannot be taken over by the abstract terminology of *analogia entis*, which reduces the concrete Christological centre of faith to Scholastic metaphysics. Balthasar's own Christocentrism, learned from another great Jesuit mentor, Henri de Lubac, made him sympathetic to this objection. But he proposed to answer it *not* by abandoning the *analogia entis* but by reformulating the analogy of being idea in such a way as to show how it could serve, rather than substitute for, a Christological account of the creation-covenant. Jesus Christ, Balthasar proposed, is *the concrete analogy of being in person.*[91]

This was of assistance when Balthasar turned to write the theological aesthetics. In his book on Barth he had already invoked the idea of Christ's *form* – the key term of the aesthetics – in just this context of analogy. He had agreed with Barth that Christ cannot be regarded as simply an instance of a Creator-creature analogy established independently of him, since on the unique form of the God-man – the Christ-form – depends 'the form of the creation that has emerged from him, from whom it takes its being'[92]. After all, man, the microcosm of the world, is made, in Old Testament thinking, in the image of God, a statement the New Testament evaluates by reference to the supreme icon that is Christ. And since Christ '*is* his own form', the form of his revelation, then, turns on nothing but himself.[93] As Balthasar explains in Volume I of *The Glory of the Lord*, only Christ, as both divine Son and human being, can express absolute Being within a worldly form.[94] Only Christ is the 'measure' between God and man.[95] He is the 'hypostatic union between archetype [God] and image [man]'[96]. Through the elevation of his created nature by the grace of union, expressed in practice by Jesus' perfect obedience to the Father, the humanity of Christ is raised up to have a common measure with the Word's measure. In this marvellous accord, he becomes as man the active expression of God.

We notice, however, that this appeal to the uniqueness of Christ in the aesthetics is not by way of *replacing* analogy thinking. On the contrary, the appearance of revelation *presupposes* an analogical relation between God's being and created being. There must be some similarity as well as dissimilarity between them, or else revelation could not be seen, or indeed occur at all. In terms of theological aesthetics with its characteristic 'form thinking', to say that Christ is the 'concrete analogy of being' means that the hypostatic union furnishes the supreme form of the relation between God and creature. And since Jesus is the 'Trinitarian Son', the Son who can only be defined by his relations with Father and with Spirit, that 'analogy', which he as the God-man personally is, furnishes the form that discloses the Trinitarian relationships both in themselves and in relation to the world. Through the Incarnation which makes Christ the concrete *analogia entis* in person, the relation between God and creation, properly described in the analogy of being, is caught up into the inner-Trinitarian relations. Or, as Balthasar himself puts it:

*The relation between God and creature
in this way comes to participate in the
natural indissolubility of the love
between the Father and the Son in the
Holy Spirit.*[97]

But further progress in considering how the concrete analogy, Jesus Christ, makes his impact on us could not be achieved without turning from aesthetics to dramatics with its key-word, 'freedom'.

The Christological 'analogy of freedom'

Theological dramatics considers the material content which has come to formal expression in theological aesthetics, the content that is not an object to be looked at so much as it is, in Balthasar's words, 'God's action in and upon the world'[98]. As long ago as his Barth book, Balthasar had clearly surmised that he would have to find yet a further extension of analogy thinking to cope with this fact. As he put it there, in words that neatly express, years in advance, the transition from the aesthetics to the dramatics:

*The Son of God did not become man solely to
represent and to be the definitive analogy
between God and the creature in general
terms. His mission was more concrete than
that: he took on the form of the concrete
analogy between the God of wrath and
grace and between the creature both
condemned and redeemed.*[99]

What is added here to the perspective Balthasar will adopt in theological aesthetics is the sense of *conflict-ridden mission*, appropriate to a fallen world, which will dominate the theological dramatics. Christ's analogical character as the union of God and man cannot be described as entirely comprehensive *unless it encompasses the drama of redemption*. Quite rightly, Balthasar spends a great deal of time in *Theo-drama* on Christ's atoning work which is where his mission, as the Son sent from the Father for our good, comes fully into its own. Here the *analogia entis* becomes what Balthasar calls in the dramatics the *analogia libertatis*, the 'analogy of freedom': the analogy, namely, between divine freedom and human freedom, between the freedom which makes possible dramatic action within the Godhead, and the freedom which makes possible the human drama on earth. This is not something completely other than the analogy of being, because in freedom we are concerned with a mode of being, one expression of ontology. But it does mean that, compared with the analogy of being as hitherto generally understood, or even when understood by Balthasar as an expression of the difference-yet-attunement between two Christ's natures in the hypostatic union, analogy now takes on a dramatic character that is salvific for the world.

So what Balthasar now wants to assert is that, as he writes in the second volume of the dramatics: 'the relationship between uncreated and created freedom ... is the concrete thrust of the *analogia entis*'[100]. Just as the analogy of being was made concrete in the Incarnation, previewed in the world's creation which always, 'before' time began, had the Incarnation in mind, so now that concretised analogy fuller realised in Christ is to be made yet more concrete still in the analogy of free activity, the *analogia libertatis*.

In the theological dramatics, Balthasar assembles and develops a number of relevant considerations from his earlier works. In the theological aesthetics, he had claimed that since the light of faith respects human freedom, the engracement of the created subject so takes place that his or her freedom is likewise respected. Since Balthasar could hardly write a theological aesthetics without considering the nature of the act of the faith (the Christian version of aesthetic perception), it was inevitable that he should to some degree anticipate there, even if obliquely, the topics he would handle fully and head-on in the dramatics. In Catholic theology, the act of faith, considered as a properly human action, rather than the effect of divine agency, is essentially free. Hence Balthasar had included a little excursus on the topic of freedom and obedience even in the aesthetics. In the words of one student of the freedom theme in Balthasar's corpus:

> *If one says 'Yes' in belief to the light of*
> *God's glory as it shines out of the Christ-*
> *form, that act of self-surrender or*
> *obedience is understood by Balthasar to*
> *be a liberation or perfection of one's*
> *freedom and a participation in the very*
> *freedom of Christ which he lives as*
> *obedience so that the beauty of God's*
> *love might be revealed to the world.*[101]

Despite these anticipations, however, it is only in the dramatics that this theme really takes off. The mere existence of finite freedom, so Balthasar maintains in *Theo-drama*, implies a 'natural' dramatic relationship between God and the world on the basis of creation. But when God sends his Son, a new 'acting area' – a new arena for action – is opened up in the created world. Its distinctive feature is that *finite freedom can now be inserted into infinite freedom*. Christ as actor mediates the divine author's plan for humanity along these lines. Now it transpires that, in Thomas Dalzell's words, the

> *ultimate horizon which gives meaning*
> *to human dramatic existence is not just*
> *absolute Being ... but trinitarian Being*
> *understood as interpersonal freedom in*
> *God.*[102]

For Balthasar, an adequate grasp of that 'horizon', which seen most deeply is not just triune freedom but triune love, is only available if full justice is done to the significance of the event of the Cross, with its issue in Easter and Pentecost. In the Resurrection, theo-dramatically conceived, the natural acting area which exists by virtue of creation becomes an 'area' for action that extends right into heaven – indeed, right into the heart of the Trinity itself, while acceptance of the Holy Spirit's Pentecost mission enables individuals to enter into Christ's acting area and so into the inter-action of the divine persons themselves. When the Christ who personalises the analogy of being in his own ontological constitution goes on to encompass not just the meta-physical structure of the God-creature relation but also the situation in history of the relation between God and sinners, then his concrete analogy takes the form of the Paschal Mystery, the Cross and Resurrection. And this, his self-giving to the Father for creatures and notably guilty creatures, is the redemption of the world. The analogy of being, now enhanced as the analogy of freedom, comes to its consummation as a trinitarian life in Christ.[103]

From 'analogy of freedom' to 'analogy of charity'

This raises the question of what happens to the analogy of being in the analogy of freedom when it finds expression in life in Christ. How does the analogy of liberty look in the practice of the Christian life, which is at once a moral life and a mystical life: an ascetic struggle with evil in the vices and a transfigura-tion of all our virtualities by grace? To Balthasar's eyes, human sin is a blindness to the proper relation between God and man, a relation expressed in the analogy of being with its provision for both likeness and dissimilarity. In the case of sinful man, anal-ogy becomes instability, or what Balthasar terms a 'sliding between nothingness and infinity'[104]. The polarities operative in human nature – between matter and spirit, and between man as microcosm and the wider macrocosm of nature, between male and female, and individual and community, analysed at length as these are in the second volume of the dramatics – point man beyond himself to find fulfilment in God.[105] When not distorted by sin, such polarity can serve as an analogy for the inner-Trinitarian relations: if humankind is made in the image of God the Word, who was made incarnate as Jesus Christ, it is made in the image of the Trinitarian Son – and hence in the image of the Trinity. But once polarity is disturbed, it generates indefinitely many distortions in human living. Their characteristic final upshot, on Balthasar's analysis of sin, is to immerse people either in hubristic delusions of grandeur or in deeply disordered despair.[106] But through his Cross and Resurrection the incarnate Son:

> *returns the analogy to its source within*
> *the Godhead by redeeming sinful man,*
> *and so becomes the concrete form of*
> *Christian life, to be followed and*
> *imitated.*[107]

The Christian life is a participation in that redemption. That participation requires for its understanding the third and last form of analogy – the analogy of love.

In its new form, the *analogia entis* within the *analogia libertatis* calls forth from Balthasar a third version of analogy thinking which we can term with the German student of his thought Manfred Lochbrunner: *analogia caritatis*, the 'analogy of charity'[108]. The Christian is called to be the analogous expression of the charity of God in Jesus Christ. In the process of accepting a mission 'in Christ' in the space opened out by Christ's extension of the theo-drama into his Church, the Christian man or woman becomes – in an analogous sense (what else?!) – 'Eucharistic', 'shared out with Christ as nourishment for the Mystical Body'[109]. As Lochbrunner's Belgian counterpart Georges de Schrijver puts it:

> *In offering himself in obedience ... the*
> *Christian becomes the means of expression*
> *and the language which God uses to*
> *proclaim his kenosis of love.*[110]

This is the greatest goodness, the goodness of being a saint. It is also what freedom was finally meant to be. Hence Balthasar's consuming interest in the lives of the saints, and in the theology of sanctity – not least as expressed in imaginative writers such as, in France, Georges Bernanos and, in Germany, Reinhold Schneider on both of whom he wrote comprehensive studies.[111]

Does the drama of salvation enrich God?

Evidently, the message of the dramatics is that we are to increase in goodness but is it possible also to say that the goodness of the God who is himself wholly actual perfection can be augmented too? In the theological dramatics, Balthasar offers an understanding of the Holy Trinity in relation to creation which goes beyond anything to be found in classical Catholic thought. In the final volume of the dramatics, Balthasar claims he has found a way of speaking about the relation between God and the world as a relation in which the world not only receives from God but also gives to him. He has found, he thinks, a way of speaking for such divine receiving which nonetheless preserves the transcendence of God, itself the overriding concern of authors for whom it is very definitely *not* appropriate to speak of the creation as 'giving to' the Creator at all. And this is so, Balthasar claims, even though the divine receiving amounts to an *enrichment of God* – the very thing earlier theologians considered utterly incompatible with God's perfection and completeness of actuality. In his dramatics Balthasar comes to this conclusion by exploring how creation's encounter with God is an active participation in the encounter eternally eventuating in God between the Father, the Son and the Holy Spirit.

To grasp this we need to look at how Balthasar understands the immanent Trinity, the Trinity in itself. Balthasar's conception of the inner life of God turns, quite rightly, on God's self-revelation in the economy found in saving history. Taking his categories, as we have seen, from the world of theatre, Balthasar understands the history of salvation as a drama that reveals an eternal play: the inner-Trinitarian divine existence. There is in God an eternal drama, taking place between the

Father and the Son, the distance between them guarded yet bridged by the Holy Spirit in whom the unity of communion of the Three is secured. On the topic of 'distance': classical theology would prefer to speak here of a *distinction,* simply, but Balthasar needs a word that suggests how what is achieved by distinction is 'otherness', itself a precondition for the possibility of sacrificial loving union. On the topic of the Holy Spirit as unifying: one might think here of the Trinitarian endings of the collects of the Roman Liturgy: where the Son is said to 'live and reign, world without end, with the Father in the unity of the Holy Spirit, *in unitate Spiritus Sancti*'. (That, incidentally, was a thought especially dear to St Augustine.)

This Trinitarian 'event' is, for Balthasar, the drama that spills over into the economy through the free engagement of God for man's salvation, where the nexus of relations that constitutes the divine Trinity intersects with the world. Balthasar develops an account of the immanent Trinity where the Father communicates himself eternally to the Son, giving away his own divinity and only possessing it again in that gift, while the Son, for his part, exists as responsiveness to the Father, in an eternal saying 'thank you', *Danksagung*, for the gift he has received. Here the Holy Spirit is the mutual love of Father and Son (that is straightforward Augustinian teaching), but he is also (and this is more distinctively Balthasarian) the fruitfulness of that mutual love. He is, we might say, efficacious loving unity in person. In this presentation of the eternal inter-personal life of the Trinity as kenotic self-communication, Balthasar was deeply influenced by the Russian Orthodox dogmatician Sergei Bulgakov, who stresses the self-emptying character of all the Trinitarian processions.[112]

One of the tasks of theologians is to criticise each other's work in the name not only of intellectual coherence but also of faithfulness to Tradition. The late Père Bertrand de Margerie, of the Society of Jesus, from a position of basic sympathy with Balthasar's work, put several pertinent questions along these lines, fearing that, despite Balthasar's obviously orthodox intention, 'a kind of human psychologism' risked drawing him 'in the direction of tritheism'[113]. There are three ideas in Balthasar's theology of the immanent Trinity that de Margerie finds objectionable. The first is the notion that the Son 'allows himself to be generated'[114], as though two distinct divine wills were involved. But in God there is only one will, that of the only God. Since, however, we should surely presume Balthasar was not so foolish as to suppose the Son could act before he was originated, I think we must take this as a colourful statement of the Son's acknowledgement of his total dependence on the Father for receiving the divine nature. The same is true of de Margerie's second objection, a related criticism of Balthasar's account of the procession of the Spirit. The Spirit, for Balthasar, 'acquiesces' in his joint spiration by Father and by Son.[115] I take that to mean, again, the Holy Spirit acknowledges his total dependence on those who breathe him forth. De Margerie also, with more warrant this time, objects to the language of 'separation' which Balthasar's theology of the otherness within the Trinity leads him to use in relation to Father and Son. Accepting that Balthasar puts the term 'separation' into scare-quotes, de Margerie can find no place for it in the vocabulary of Trinitarian theology, and cites approvingly Cardinal Walter Kasper's statement in his *The God of Jesus Christ* to the effect that, even on the Cross, there is between the divine Persons infinitely more interrelation than there ever is between human persons, owing to their unity. To use 'separation' as a synonym for infinite distinction is certainly odd (even more so than to speak of 'distance'), but Balthasar would not actually quarrel with Kasper's statement. He would see it, rather, as true by virtue of a covert reference, in the relations of Father and Son, to the role of the Holy Spirit. There remains to mention, in de Margerie's critique, his allergy to the entire vocabulary of renunciation and sacrifice in the relations of origin and communion, a vocabulary Balthasar drew from Bulgakov. His objection was anticipated by earlier Catholic theologians when considering the claims of the Russian dogmaticians before the Second Vatican Council: for instance, the Flemish

Dominican Edward Schillebeeckx in his more obviously orthodox and Thomist phase. In *Christ the Sacrament* Schillebeeckx
wrote sharply:

> *only in his human existence can the Son's eternal*
> *giving of himself to the Father be realised in the true*
> *form of a sacrifice and of self-dispossession.*[116]

Nor would Schillebeeckx accept even the milder language of
dependence at least in what he termed the 'strict meaning of the
word'. Only with the Incarnation does the Son's intimacy of life
with the Father take on the character of dependence. For the first
time, in Schillebeeckx's words, 'dependence now enters the
relation of love'[117]. We can note, however, that the same writer
had no objection at all to the language of 'perfect active receptivity' which, a generation later, Balthasar would make his own.[118]
I note that de Margerie did not comment on what has struck
many readers as the strangest aspect of Balthasar's theology of
the immanent Trinity in the theodramatics, and this is what may
be called the gender fluidity of his theology of the divine persons
– though the point of this is precisely to underline issues of
'perfect active receptivity', in Schillebeeckx's phrase. In the
fourth volume of the theological dramatics, Balthasar presents
the Son as feminine in relation to the Father's masculinity, yet
Father and Son as masculine in jointly spirating the initially
feminine Spirit, while the Father too can be said to be feminine is
receiving the processions back into himself from Spirit and Son.
In other words, all the persons for Balthasar are both masculine
and feminine in different respects. Evidently, what Balthasar is
trying to do is to express the ways in which the divine persons
both initiate and receive in their eternal constitution as God.[119]
De Margerie would say that Balthasar's mistake is to fashion the
immanent Trinity too much in the image of humanity, by
neglecting the demands of the *via negativa* and the *via eminen-
tiae* which are integral aspects of the doctrine of analogy to
which, in principle, Balthasar was committed.

Balthasar's theology of the immanent Trinity in *Theo-drama* is a powerful reading which takes with utmost seriousness the claim of St John's first Letter that 'God is love', understanding this as the renunciatory yet joyous love typical of willing sacrifice, a love which reached its lowest – yet highest – pitch on the Cross. Balthasar interprets the divine essence, the divine originating processions of Son and Spirit, and the entire life of communion of the divine persons in their reciprocal possession of the divine nature, from this very standpoint. He does so not over against an ontology of the Trinitarian life – this is not an alternative to a Christian metaphysic, but by way of providing such an ontology, it is a gloss on a Christian metaphysic. For Balthasar, investigation of the mystery of being already alerts us to how being is gift, *it gives itself away*.[120] Classical theology enquires into the being of the Trinity, in its single substance, and threefold personhood; Balthasar considered he was doing the same. In the view of some, however, Balthasar's enthusiasm for the key notion of divine self-giving leads him to overstep the bounds of theological propriety, which are the bounds of any theological discourse that is controlled not only by Scripture but also by the intrinsic demands of letting God be God.

For Balthasar, God's love is a dynamic exchange between hypostases. To describe this love, we need not only the concepts appropriate to metaphysical thought but metaphors too. He accepts that metaphor applied to divine substance can run wild. This is why metaphor profits by a discipline of correction from metaphysical thinking about God where negative theology can be brought in to control, when the need arises, the assertions of its affirmative counterpart. The question of divine enhancement through God's own relations with the world in creation and salvation is comparable in this respect to the question of sacrifice or suffering in God, and – a more distinctively Balthasarian theme – 'surprise' in God. We have already touched on the question of divine sacrifice (and hence, suffering or, rather, 'suffering' – since only analogy connects suffering in the creaturely realm with renunciation in God). As the brilliant Irish student of Balthasar's thought Thomas Dalzell sums up:

> *The emptying of the Father's heart in letting*
> *the Son proceed is taken to be the eternal*
> *presupposition and pre-eminent instance of*
> *possible suffering, alienation and pain in the*
> *world.*[121]

Balthasar rules out worldly-type suffering in the Blessed Trinity. God does not suffer in the way we do. Yet in God there is something like suffering – not, however, suffering as an evil (here we find Balthasar invoking a negative truth so as to protect an appropriate metaphysic of the divine being), but rather the suffering – again, I should prefer to write 'suffering' – involved in kenotic love. Nonetheless, Balthasar imagines an event – the aboriginal 'event' of the divine processions – in God which 'lays the foundation for all possible suffering in the world and the participation of God in it'[122]. This may suggest an ancient heresy, but as an American commentator notes:

> *The term 'kenosis' is not meant to be interpreted*
> *in a patripassianist sense, but as dramatic dynamism:*
> *The Father 'is this movement of self-giving that holds*
> *nothing back'.*[123]

Balthasar's discussion of the notion of divine surprise – more specifically, the Father's surprise at the Son – is more obviously indebted to metaphor. Once again there is an attempt to go beyond the limits of negative theology in order to evoke, in this case, the *liveliness* of the triune love. In Dalzell's words, Balthasar's

> *recourse to metaphor to speak about the*
> *Father's surprise at the Son's response [to*
> *him] is an attempt to say something about*
> *the Father's joy at the extent of the Son's*
> *self-gift …*[124]

or, more widely, about the greatness and liveliness of their loving interaction. Presumably, negative theology would rule out the attribution to God of wonder and surprise should these words be taken at face value. In the context of the immanent Trinity, that caveat would be entered on the ground of the oneness of knowledge and freedom of Father and Son. For Balthasar, each of the three persons is certainly conscious and free. This, however, is a matter of Father, Son and Holy Spirit each operating in his own way on the basis of the single divine consciousness and freedom rooted as these are in the single divine essence. Yet none of this rules out the metaphorical depiction, in these contested terms, of the Father's superabundant delight in the person of the Son.

On the specific issue of the 'enrichment' of God: as Dalzell, again, points out, this needs to be contextualised in Balthasar's account of God's inner-trinitarian love as a dynamic, everintensifying self-enrichment. It is not that the eternal exchange between the persons is in any way deficient, or that its loveexchange has anything of the merely potential about it. Rather is its perfect actuality ever-renewed in a fashion that can indeed be called 'intensifying'. In his early study of the Cappadocian theologian Gregory of Nyssa, Balthasar had drawn on St Gregory's image of the divine being as a fountain whose water returns constantly to its source in an ongoing circular dynamic[125], an image which may, I believe, have struck him with particular force since it recurs, as an expression of livingness, in the German poets. In the third volume of the dramatics, Balthasar makes it plain that he considers divine substance *as possessed by the Trinitarian persons* to perdure in an *Überzeit*, 'supra-time', conceived as a medium for the loving inter-action of Father, Son and Spirit, in fountain-like fashion. As Balthasar presents things, in the dialogue of love between Father and Son, the Holy Spirit is

> *forever showing to each new possibilities for*
> *their self-gift to each other and so further*
> *delight as new expectations are surpassed.*[126]

In this connexion the Holy Spirit represents the 'exuberance', *Überschwang*, and 'surplus', *Überfluss*, of the triune love. The dynamic in God has not ended with the Son's giving himself back to the Father in the moment of acknowledging his eternal generation. While that dynamic is in one sense already complete and perfect, in another sense it is forever coming to be. For Balthasar this does not contradict the eternal actuality of God. Since in his own nature God is absolute freedom he can allow ever new aspects of himself to appear even within the exchange of the divine persons.

The question of divine enrichment – more specifically by creatures and notably by creatures both redeemed and sanctified – is the question of whether we can describe the total process of the world's salvation through homecoming to the Trinity as inserted into the content of such 'supra-time'. For Balthasar, the world enters God through participation in the otherness of the eternal Son. When in time the incarnate Son returns to the Father in the Paschal Mystery, he takes the world with him – without overpowering anyone's freedom – into the exchange of love in God going on for ever in supra-time. In this way the human being becomes not a spectator (an unfortunate, if unintended, connotation of the more usual language of 'beatific vision') but a participant in the 'streaming life of God.[127] Balthasar has already argued that God's love is not only something already perfectly given and received but as including, in the triune life, an eternal increase. Now, encouraged by such biblical images of mutuality as the banquet of heaven or the eschatological wedding feast, he wants to say that while God's inner life of love is always plenary, its 'ever-greater' dimensions can make room for a contribution from the world. In language that shocks more sober theological thinkers (and indebted to his mystical associate, Adrienne von Speyr – never far away when Balthasarian audacities are in view[128]), Balthasar speaks of an 'enrichment', *Bereicherung*, of heaven; a 'becoming ever-richer', *Je-reicher-werden*, of the Trinity; an 'embellishment', *Ausschmückung*, of the Father's richness. These are metaphors. But Balthasar holds that in this case the use of metaphors can bring us closer to the truth than the use of concepts alone. What appears to be the 'addition' to God he has in mind is in no sense a condition for the absolute divine perfection, guarded by negative theology, and so in no way implies deficiency in God. I say, 'what appears to be the addition', because in actual fact what the world gives to God, as Balthasar makes clear, is what *it gives back to God of the love it has received in taking part in the Trinitarian dialogue,* through the saving economy in which God himself has enfolded it. The motto is, in the words of the Liturgy of St John Chrysostom, 'Thine of thy own we offer to thee'.

The dramatic dénouement: Balthasar's eschatology

I said that the dénouement of theodrama for Balthasar lies in the homecoming of the world to God through the enfolding of creation in the triune life. Classically, that is the subject we call 'eschatology' – at any rate in eschatology's sheerly positive aspect, the life of heaven. We can usefully consider Balthasar's eschatology – his account of the consummated good for man – in terms of first, the Church; secondly, the individual; thirdly, the world.

First, then, the Church. The confident dogmatic tone of Balthasar's account of the world's homecoming to the Trinity and his profound hope that all may be saved might lead us to think that his evaluation of the fortunes of the community that carries God's plan must be a highly positive one. The inference would be mistaken. Balthasar's prognosis for the future of the Church in the short and middle terms was pessimistic. True, he rejected the suggestion of the French poet and social commentator Charles Péguy to the effect that there is in history a *communio peccatorum*, energised by the Devil and working to undermine the *communio sanctorum* achieved by Christ. Balthasar considered that evil is essentially divisive and isolating and thus unable to create communion of any kind even for common nefarious purposes. Nonetheless, he noted, the Church is in competition with an increasingly self-confident secular world-culture with universal aspirations of its own, the origins of which go back, so Balthasar thought, to the Roman principate of Caesar Augustus. (That, he surmised, shows the providential reason why the Word became incarnate at the time he did.) Secular universal enlightenment in Balthasar's view is now found within the Church as well as outside it (an example would be the influence wielded by the work of Hans Küng of Tübingen, a typical Enlightenment thinker). In much modern theology, spirituality, catechesis, the full Gospel, Balthasar feared, is so attenuated as to be in danger of disappearing altogether.

Balthasar's negative prognosis was based partly, then, on a reading of the state of the contemporary Catholic Church. But it was not restricted to observation. It also appealed to an interpretation of Scripture and certain elements in the later Tradition which encouraged him to think of history moving into a more polarised world/Church conflict as we draw closer to the Eschaton, and not, as some twentieth-century Church documents (like the Pastoral Constitution of the Second Vatican Council on the Church in the Modern World) might lead us to think, a less polarised one.[129] Of course Balthasar was no pessimist in regard to the ultimate future of the Church, for that future is secured in the Resurrection of the Saviour. But in the interim the Church must act and struggle on the world-stage. Balthasar offered his theodramatics, and in different ways the rest of his theology, come to that, as shining armour for this spiritual warfare.

Turning now to Balthasar's Christian hope for individuals, critics ask whether, despite his protestations, he is committed to universalism, the view that all persons shall be saved. Balthasar wrote two short popular books on this topic, where he makes it plain that his proposal is that we may *hope* that all will be saved, even though we can neither teach it as doctrine nor hold it as certain in our capacity as individual members of the Church.[130] But some would say the way he speaks about Christ's descent into Hell as a victory in every sense over sin, as well as death, in effect makes the universalist outcome of the drama of salvation more than just something we might hope for without actually knowing, with the certitude of faith, that it will come to pass. How can Balthasar say God does not take humanity's 'No' as final, and still allow for the human freedom to go to Hell?

What, if anything, did Balthasar's eschatology have to say about the ultimate future of the wider social context of the individual-civil society? More self-consciously contemporary theologians are concerned about the lack of *social content* to Balthasar's presentation of ultimate human destiny. For when modern theologians consider eschatology, both in its future and also in its realised or incipient aspect, they want some assurance that what is being said has relevance to civil society. This is in part a reflection of the hyper-inflation of politics in the modern era and the more general flight from the eternal to the temporal which typifies societies strongly influenced by materialism, both philosophical and economic. But it also reflects a genuine concern of the tradition, namely that the *telos* of natural society should be included within any account of human destiny. After all, eschatology is about the consummation of the created order as a whole.

Balthasar is certainly more interested in the destiny of persons than in that of the social totality. His particular version of eschatology takes its marching orders from his account of how the personal identity of human beings relates to the eternal procession and mission of the divine Son. St Thomas had already taught that the mission of Christ is a prolongation of his eternal procession. Balthasar holds strongly to the unity of the procession and the mission of the Son. For him, this unity grounds the thesis that the 'idea' of any human being – what God fundamentally makes of them – comes forth in the Son in such a way that it is simultaneously the 'idea' of one's mission in Christ. When created freedom responds to God in me or you, it becomes a participation in the 'readiness', *Bereitschaft*, of the Son: his ever-greater 'Yes' to being what the Father wants him to be. I exercise my freedom as a person – which for Balthasar's theological dramatics means not just an individual human being but a player in the divine drama, a *persona dramatis,* by being in relationship with the Son, sharing in his unique mission. And so Balthasar understands the ultimate end of human freedom as a taking part in God's Trinitarian life process.

The finite is already to a certain degree the realisation of its own 'idea'. Its redemption is a matter of its being enabled to realise that idea much more fully by virtue of the mediation of the incarnate Son. Its place in God is a realisation of God's idea of it, in the 'otherness' of the Son, but its full access to the inner life of God in the Son only comes about through the Resurrection of the Crucified. The Resurrection of Christ from the dead is for redeemed persons the condition and the cause of sharing in the Trinitarian exchange. The Cross and Resurrection event is, after all, the economic realisation of the Son's eternal giving himself back to the Father. Only by participating in Christ's risen humanity, then, can we ourselves be gathered into the spacious freedom of God, finding our home there in God's infinite freedom expressed as Trinitarian love. Here the natural reaching out of human freedom to God is perfected and enabled to reach its goal. The relation between the graced creature and God preserves and elevates the relation between the natural creature and God.

But it is precisely Balthasar's emphasis on the way the natural relations of the creature to the divine plan for humanity are not abolished but preserved and enhanced which leads some commentators to express astonishment at the extent of the disjuncture he makes between hopes for a better world on the one hand and the Trinitarian ingathering, *Einbergung*, of the redeemed on the other. Certainly, some weight must be given to the general theological and ecclesial situation in which Balthasar was writing. His mature work was framed by the French 'theology of earthly realities' of the immediately pre-Conciliar period, and the American 'theology of secularisation', the German 'political theology', and the Latin American 'liberation theology' of the immediately and not so immediately post-Conciliar years.

Balthasar was inclined to tar all these theologies – not entirely implausibly – with the same brush. He considered that they had replaced strictly theological hope, a hope based on the revealed divine promises, by hope as human passion, full of pathos, certainly, but to which no such grand guarantees were attached. Theological hope has been secularised, become an absolute hope principle (the reference is to the German social philosopher Ernst Bloch), cut off from its religious pole. A horizontalised pseudo-theological hope gives priority to the socio-political over the religious, to future-oriented human forms of practice over God's practice towards us. And apart from the sheer unfoundedness of the Utopianism that resulted, it also led people to relativise and eventually to lose from consciousness altogether the divine achievement already present in the Church by virtue of the Resurrection of Christ.

It is suggested that Balthasar's strong – some would say allergic – reaction to these theologies is an over-reaction which led him to positions not fully compatible with his own principles. Although he does, it is true, place more emphasis on the way grace liberates and transforms human freedom, in the manner of Augustine, he also recognises the truth of the Greek patristic position that human freedom has its own autonomous structure apart from grace and certainly not in essential opposition to grace. If he had wanted, he could have produced a more generous account, then, of the human 'passion of hope'; than he did. One thinks for example of the version of that in a philosopher-dramatist Balthasar admired, the French Existentialist Gabriel Marcel.

Again, just as in the theological aesthetics, Balthasar privileged, so it would seem, the 'forms', 'gestalts', of individual realities, whereas he could, had he wished, have included social forms, the forms that show themselves in social communion, in a monastic community, say, or a well-ordered polis, so in the theological dramatics there is a lack of social drama. Refusing to apply his account of the nature-grace relationship to the social plane, as distinct from the inter-personal one, he missed an opportunity to bring his dramatics into possibly fruitful dialogue with social theology.

These charges can in decent part be answered. First of all, it is difficult to see how someone can be regarded as an out-and-out personalist for whom the communitarian dimension of life is under-appreciated when they have made the concept of communion – *communio* – so crucial to their theology of the Church in the light of their theology of God. (He called his theological journal *Communio*, for goodness' sake!) What is more true is that Balthasar did not believe communitarianism could ever trump personalism. Possibly owing to his background in Ignatian spirituality, personal conversion is key for him. The Christian enjoys fellowship with God in Christ in the midst of the Church, and yet only individual persons can be the subjects of such fellowship, such enjoyment. Particular persons bulk extremely large in Balthasar's vision: St John the Evangelist, St Ignatius, Adrienne von Speyr. In the dramatics, so it has been said:

> *[Balthasar] was not interested in a general*
> *resemblance of the human to the divine, but*
> *rather in the individual subject exercising his*
> *or her freedom to enter into correspondence*
> *with God.*[131]

Again, that is only partly just, as Balthasar's lengthy discussion of the traditional basis of Christian anthropology in the doctrine of man 'made to God's image and likeness' makes clear. That basis gives him a universal theological anthropology, turning on the biblical motif most used by the Fathers and later theologians for exactly that general purpose. Possibly, however, the way Balthasar uses the analogy of being tends to stress the ways *individual persons* realise concretely their fundamental human identity in God's likeness. Owing to his emphasis on the concreteness of analogy – not only the analogy of being but also the analogy of freedom and the analogy of charity, Balthasar is working with what the Scholastics called an analogy of proportionality, which relates one relationship to another relationship owing to the similar proportions in each. In the theological dramatics, just as the incarnate Son chooses a self-transcendence that corresponds to the self-transcendence of the Father, so the individual person chooses to accept God in Jesus Christ as the law or norm of his or her life. The similar proportions involved are, therefore, similar proportions in *one-to-one relationships*. Rather different is the analogy of attribution which is based on the likeness to some one thing of many things, thus pointing up the commonalities running through creation – in a textbook example, the 'health' in a healthy body, a healthy diet, a healthy appetite, healthy exercise, healthy reading material. That would suggest that, on this point, Balthasar's theology cannot be 'rectified' by a little judicious supplementation here and there. His theology is not set up in a way that is likely to be helpful if what is wanted is an account of *social* expressions of divine likeness (other than the family). For that, other theologies must be brought into play. In Catholicism no one theology – especially if it is that of a single genius, rather than a school can serve exclusively all the Church's needs in bringing her vision to expression.[132] This takes us neatly enough to the final contribution to the great trilogy, Balthasar's theological logic, which corresponds to the analogate 'true'.

72   *Theo-drama. Theological Dramatic Theory. I: Prolegomena* (San Francisco, Ignatius, 1988).

73   'Balthasar's Christ-centredness and Spirit-centredness are ultimately directed to the centre that is the Father', J. Naduvilekut, *Christus der Heilsweg: Soteria als Theodrama im Werk Hans Urs von Balthasars* (Sankt Ottilien, Eos Verlag, 1987), p. 382.

74   *Mysterium Paschale*, op. cit., pp. vii–ix.

75   B. F. Meyer, *Christus Faber. The Master-Builder of the House of God* (Allison Park, PS, Pickwick, 1992), p. 2.

76   A. Birot, ' "God in Christ, Reconciled the World to Himself": Redemption in Balthasar', *Communio* 24 (1997), pp. 259–285, and here at p. 282.

77   R. A. Howsare, *Balthasar*, op. cit., p. 117.

78 *Theo-drama. Theological Dramatic Theory IV. The Action* (San Francisco, Ignatius, 1994).

79 H. Steinhauer, *Maria als dramatische Person bei Hans Urs von Balthasar. Zum marianischen Prinzip seines Denkens* (Innsbruck-Vienna, Tyrolia Verlag, 2001).

80 H. U. von Balthasar – J. Ratzinger, *Mary: the Church at the Source* (San Francisco, Ignatius, 2005).

81 F. A. Murphy, 'Desacralized Time and Progress', *Second Spring* 2 (2002), pp. 50–51. Professor Murphy's criticisms of 'narrative theology' were subsequently greatly expanded in *God is Not a Story. Realism Revisited* (Oxford, Oxford University Press, 2007), where she argued that the emphasis on language – its 'grammar', and the method involved in its proper use – characteristic of those theologically concerned with story tends to marginalise event: compare her prediction that 'in relation to the Church, the Trinity, and even eschatology we will find that narrative theology draws back from engagement with the temporality of human events', ibid., p. 15.

82 For Balthasar's use of this work in his earliest magnum opus, *Apokalypse der deutschen Seele*, see A. Nichols, O. P., *Scattering the Seed. A Guide through Balthasar's early Writings on Philosophy and the Arts* (London, T. & T. Clark, 2006), p. 72.

83 D. J. Potter, 'Post-Kantian Idealism and the Dramas of Schiller and Zacharias Werner with Principal Reference to the Period 1800 to 1810', Doctoral dissertation of the University of Cambridge (1992), pp. 58–59.

84 Ibid., p. 59. I am very grateful to the Revd Dr Potter for his permission to quote these two passages.

85 *Theo-drama. Theological Dramatic Theory I. Prolegomena*, op. cit., p. 125.

86 Ibid., p. 126.

87 Ibid., pp. 130–131.

88 *Theo-drama. Theological Dramatic Theory III. Dramatis Personae: Persons in Christ* (San Francisco, Ignatius, 1992), p. 525.

89 J. Neuner and J. Dupuis, (ed.), *The Christian Faith in the Doctrinal Documents of the Catholic Church* (London 1983), p. 108. The citation is of John 17:22.

90 *Theo-drama. Theological Dramatic Theory III. Dramatis Personae: Persons in Christ*, op. cit., p. 221.

91 After the writing of his Barth book, variant versions of this formula pullulate in Balthasar's work: Christ is 'the concrete analogy of being', *A Theology of History* (London, Sheed and Ward, 1964), p. 74; he is the 'analogy of being in person', *Epilog* (Einsiedeln, Johannes Verlag, 1987), p. 69.

92 *The Theology of Karl Barth. Exposition and Interpretation* (San Francisco, Ignatius, 1992), p. 55.

93 Barth would have called this an example – *the* example – of the 'analogy of faith' which for him means not (as in most Catholic theology) the coherence which holds good between various doctrines, various aspects of revelation, but, rather, analogies between creature and Creator divinely made known to us thanks to the revelation of God in Christ.

[94] *The Glory of the Lord. A Theological Aesthetic I: Seeing the Form*, op cit., p. 458.

[95] Ibid., p. 473.

[96] Ibid., p. 432.

[97] Ibid., p. 480.

[98] *Theo-Drama. Theological Dramatic Theory I. Prolegomena*, op. cit., p. 15.

[99] *The Theology of Karl Barth*, op. cit., p. 376.

[100] *Theo-drama. Theological Dramatic Theory II. Dramatis Personae: Man in God* (San Francisco, Ignatius, 1990), p. 123.

[101] T. G. Dalzell, S. M., *The Dramatic Encounter of Divine and Human Freedom in the Theology of Hans Urs von Balthasar* (Berne, Peter Lang, 1997), p. 110.

[102] Ibid., p. 127.

[103] Compare the careful formulation by Nicholas Healy: '[T]he Thomistic analogy of being, fulfilled in the person of Christ, is both the abiding precondition of, and is ultimately disclosed in, the drama between God and the world whose form takes shape within Christ's return to the Father through his being given for and into the world in the Holy Spirit'. Thus N. J. Healy, *The Eschatology of Hans Urs von Balthasar. Being as Communion* (Oxford, Oxford University Press, 2005), p. 3.

[104] *Theo-drama. Theological Dramatic Theory II. Dramatis Personae: Man in God*, op. cit., p. 406.

[105] Ibid., pp. 346–394.

[106] Ibid., pp. 359, 400. Balthasar's discussion of Pascal's thought in the third volume of *The Glory of the Lord* is relevant here.

[107] A. Franz Franks, 'Trinitarian *analogia entis* in Hans Urs von Balthasar', *The Thomist* 62 (1998), pp. 533–539, and here at p. 554.

[108] M. Lochbrunner, *Analogia caritatis. Darstellung und Deutung der Theologie Hans Urs von Balthasars* (Freiburg, Herder, 1981).

[109] *Theo-drama. Theological Dramatic Theory III. Dramatis Personae: The Person in Christ*, op. cit., pp. 527–528.

[110] G. de Schrijver, *Le merveilleux accord de l'homme et de Dieu. Etude de l'analogie de l'être chez Hans Urs von Balthasar* (Leuven, Peeters, 1983), p. 72. And since, at various levels – God as Trinity, God as Creator, God as incarnate, the redeeming Christ, the redeemed and (if we may venture the word) sub-redeeming Christian, the idea of kenosis appears throughout, we might also speak of an 'analogy of emptying' (*analogia exinanitionis*) in Balthasar's work, as does T. R. Krenski, *Passio caritatis. Trinitarische Passiologie im Werk Hans Urs von Balthasars* (Einsiedeln, Johannes Verlag, 1990), pp. 362–370.

[111] *Bernanos. An Ecclesial Existence* (San Francisco, Ignatius, 1996); *Tragedy under Grace. Reinhold Schneider on the Experience of the West* (San Francisco, Ignatius, 1997). I offer a survey of Balthasar's treatment of these figures in *Divine Fruitfulness. A Guide through Balthasar's Theology beyond the Trilogy* (London, Continuum, 2007), pp. 289–336.

[112] A. Nichols, O. P., *Wisdom from Above. A Primer in the Theology of Father Sergei Bulgakov* (Leominster, Gracewing, 2005), especially pp. 12–32; 151–165.

[113] B. de la Margerie, S. J., 'Note on Balthasar's Trinitarian Theology', *The Thomist* 64 (2000), pp. 127–130.

[114] *Theodrama. Theological Dramatic Theory V. The Last Act* (San Francisco, Ignatius, 1998), p. 245.

[115] Ibid., p. 223.

[116] Thus E. Schillebeeckx, *Christ the Sacrament of Encounter with God* (London, Sheed and Ward, 1963), p. 36.

[117] Ibid., p. 34.

[118] Ibid., p. 33.

[119] The language in which he expresses this, perhaps derived from the influence on him of Gregory of Nyssa's ascetical and mystical writings, lays him open to the charge that his forthright defence of an all-male ministerial priesthood in the twin essays 'Women Priests?' in *New Elucidations* (San Francisco, Ignatius, 1986), pp. 187–198, and 'The Uninterrupted Tradition of the Church' in Congregation for the Doctrine of the Faith, *From 'Inter insigniores' to 'Ordinatio sacerdotalis'* (Washington, U. S. National Conference of Catholic Bishops, 1998), pp. 99–166, is actually incompatible with his doctrine of God or at any rate that his doctrine of God provides an opening for the development of a view on the sacramental question quite contrary to his own convictions. See on this, however, R. A. Perarchick, *The Trinitarian Foundations of Human Sexuality as Revealed by Christ according to Hans Urs von Balthasar. The Revelatory Significance of the Male Christ and the Male Ministerial Priesthood* (Rome, 2000).

[120] Balthasar's fullest discussion of this important point is *The Glory of the Lord. A Theological Aesthetics V. Metaphysics in the Modern Age*, op. cit., pp. 613–627. Even at the level of philosophy, being points towards the doctrines of the Trinity, the Incarnation, the Atonement, and indeed to the practice of sanctity in the Church.

[121] T. G. Dalzell, 'The Enrichment of God in Balthasar's Trinitarian Eschatology', *Irish Theological Quarterly* 66 (2001), pp. 3–18, and here at p. 8. I have learned a lot from the judicious evaluation in this essay and the book by the same author also cited in this Chapter.

[122] Ibid., pp. 8–9.

[123] A. Franz Franks, 'Trinitarian *analogia entis* in Hans Urs von Balthasar', art. cit., p. 547 where she is citing *Theo-Drama. Theological Dramatic Theory IV. The Action*, op. cit., p. 320.

[124] T. G. Dalzell, 'The Enrichment of God in Balthasar's Trinitarian Eschatology', art. cit., p. 9.

[125] *Présence et Pensée. Essai sur la philosophie religieuse de Grégoire de Nysse* (Paris, Beauchesne, 1942), pp. 123–132. The link between Gregory's image and Balthasar's theologically dramatic account of the Trinitarian life is made by Dalzell in 'The Enrichment of God in Balthasar's Trinitarian Eschatology', art. cit., p. 10.

[126] Ibid., p. 11.

[127] Ibid., p. 12.

[128] Her inspirational value for his work is as great as the problems her excessive language causes his disciples: for his book-length testimony, see *First Glance at Adrienne von Speyr* (San Francisco, Ignatius, 1981).

[129] See not only the use of the Johannine Apocalypse in the opening section of the fourth volume of the dramatics, but the spiritual commentary on that text: *'Ja, Ich komme bald'. Die Endzeit im Licht der Apokalypse* (Freiburg, Informationszentrum Berufe der Kirche, 1985).

[130] *Was dürfen wir hoffen?* (Einsiedeln, Johannes Verlag, 1986; 1989); *Kleine Diskurs über die Hölle* (Ostfildern, Schwabenverlag, 1987). These were brought together in English as *Dare we Hope 'That all Men may be Saved', with a Short Discourse on Hell* (San Francisco, Ignatius, 1988).

[131] T. G. Dalzell, S. M., *The Dramatic Freedom of Divine and Human Encounter in the Theology of Hans Urs von Balthasar*, op. cit., p. 271.

[132] One of my major themes in A. Nichols, O. P., *The Shape of Catholic Theology. An Introduction to its Sources, Principles and History* (Collegeville, Liturgical Press, 1991).

Chapter Four

Key-word 'Logic':

Balthasar on the True

Introduction

Just as Jesus Christ is the central icon of the theological aesthetics, and the central protagonist in the theological dramatics, so when Balthasar set out to write his theological logic, he wanted to claim that Jesus Christ was the centre of all being as well.[133] He realised that one could not flesh out the claim that Jesus Christ was the midpoint of being without a thorough-going investigation into the relations of Christology with *ontology*, the study of reality in its fundamental pith, shape, direction.

Normally speaking, an 'ontological Christology' is simply an investigation of the reality of Christ as one personal being inhabiting two natures, divine and human, and accepting their union in himself. It is, typically, a Christology that takes with full metaphysical seriousness the affirmation of the Council of Chalcedon about Christ's two-in-one make-up, and tries to do it philosophical justice. But theologians who wanted to show how Christ was the world's heart could not be content with an ontological Christology of that restricted, though necessary, kind. They would need to show how Jesus Christ relates to the whole range of being in its cosmic sweep, in all its dimensions and depth.

The title for the last part of the trilogy – *Theo-logic* – comes from Hegel's thought considered as a synthesis of realism and idealism: in other words, an enquiry into the real as found in knowing. (As Hegel famously put it, 'thing must become think'.) Just as Hegel's logic (entitled *Die Wissenschaft der*

Logik) is the Swabian philosopher's ontology, so Balthasar's theo-logic (*Theo-Logik*) will be the Swiss theologian's, and with good reason, for it is through the Logos and his Spirit that all things are made and re-made. With Hegel, everything that is the case about the world must ultimately be grasped from the standpoint of 'absolute spirit'. This will take place in a comprehensive metaphysic, based on the way the 'absolute reason' of divine spirit comes to be as the event of the world unfolds. In contrast to Hegel, Balthasar is not so much interested in absolute reason as in unconditional love. For him, the whole story of the world has been enfolded right from the beginning in 'absolute love': the love of the Holy Spirit who, in different respects, is both the 'Initiator' of the world process and its supremely desirable 'Fruit'.[134] This is divine logic, the open secret of reality, truth laid bare.

The last sections of *Theo-logic*'s final volume will set out to show as much, by way, we could say, of retrospect. Meanwhile, each individual volume would include in its title the word 'truth'. Being, when known, *is* truth, and the ultimate condition of possibility for this lies in the fact that the truth of God is its measure. Balthasar agrees with Hegel that we must seek to give an account of the totality of the world that marries in some way Trinitarian and historical thinking.[135] His will be, like Hegel's, a truly comprehensive 'logic'. Both Balthasar and Hegel would, no doubt, be delighted were we to write the English word 'ontology' as 'onto-logic' – and in this way underpin, even at this early point in Chapter Four, my claim that the 'key-word' for 'Balthasar and the True' is indeed 'logic'. But Balthasar also disagrees with Hegel inasmuch as: firstly, Balthasar holds to a version of the 'perennial philosophy' indebted to St Thomas in particular, and secondly, makes 'logic' climax in a theology that turns on the Christian revelation of divine truth, understood as altogether irreducible to philosophy and independent of it – something that would be anathema to Hegel. Balthasar's account of 'the True' sets out from a pretty classical metaphysic in the tradition of the *philosophia perennis*, if somewhat modified by the more modern movement of thought called 'phenom-enology' (on which word something will be said in a moment). And it develops that account into a full-blooded theological logic where God's freely granted self-disclosure, received in faith, is what ultimately determines how truth looks.[136]

Furthermore, unlike Hegel, whose Trinitarianism is quite heterodox, Balthasar belongs firmly with the great *Paradôsis*. He understands the Son who says 'I am the Truth' and the Spirit whom Christ names 'the Spirit of truth', in terms furnished by the orthodox faith, in accordance with the Tradition of the Church. Balthasar's ontological understanding of truth by no means excludes concern for the truth of the propositions in which that ontology finds expression in right judgments, not least in dogma.

The truth of the world

The first volume of the eventual *Theo-Logic* saw the light of day in 1947 under the title 'Truth. Truth of the World'.[137] Offering the reading public an overview of his work in 1955, Balthasar gave as its purpose to 'open *philosophical* access to the specifi-cally Christian understanding of truth'[138]. For once, he did not approach the matter in a historical frame of mind (though Thomas Aquinas, and notably his *Disputed Questions on Truth*, is never far away). Launched on an adventure of constructive philosophising, Balthasar wanted to present truth in two inter-related guises. They are, respectively, phenomenological and ontological. We have already come across the word 'ontology', at the very start of this study. 'Phenomenology' is a new one in these pages, but however hard to get one's tongue around it may be, it should not baffle us. Quite simply, phenomenology may be defined as the study of the appearance of things (to our minds, as well as to – and more especially, through – our senses), so long as we add that we do not mean by that their *mere* appearance as if it were perfectly normal for things to be, as in *Alice in Wonder-land,* quite at odds with what they seem. Actually, the contrary is the case. Except in rather anormal circumstances (conjuring, *trompe l'oeil* effects in painting, and suchlike), we know things as they *appear* to us, and in this appearing it is *really they* that make themselves thus known. And how widely do things range, how richly do they display themselves! Phenomenology is a way back to ontology, from out of the cul-de-sac that is empiricism: the exaggerated worship of the isolated sense-datum. So Balthasar will consider truth *both* in its appearance to subjects (and in this perspective 'Truth of the World' is a phenomenological account of reality) *and* in its undergirding of all such appearing (and thus the book also goes beyond phenomenological description to become ontology in the proper sense of that word).

As the opening chapter of this book took pains to underline, we may start out on our enquiry from the standpoint of the perceiving subject, but that subject, for Balthasar, is aboriginally bound to being as a whole. To query the human capacity for recognising truth in all its amplitude is to cut off the branch on which the members of our race are sitting. Augustine had long ago identified the Achilles' heel of the ancient Sceptics, who, self-contradictorily, held that they at least knew that nothing can be known. In actuality, we are, in human existence, knowingly solidary with a whole host of beings that surround us, the seemingly unlimited ways in which being can be. Balthasar was well aware that what I called in Chapter One his epistemological optimism and ontological realism constitute (shades of Chesterton again) the philosophy of the common man. Reason ceases to be reasonable when it excludes or even doubts the legitimacy of such basic trust in the truth of being. In fact, such trust enables reason to function: Balthasar rejects the very concept of an autonomous reason indebted to nothing.

The aim of *Theo-logic* is not fully grasped, however, until its ultimately *theological* purpose is apprehended. The aspects of truth it covers converge on the shared knowledge and love made available in the Incarnation, when an infinite truth took on finite form (compare Chapter Two, above), and on the consequent participation of human beings in the mystery of the Trinitarian life, where the truth sets them finally free (compare Chapter Three). The second and third volumes, entitled 'Truth of God' and 'The Spirit of Truth', will, in their respective ways bring this out. Of course they could draw on the resources Balthasar had already identified in the theological aesthetics and dramatics. Basically, Balthasar focuses on four aspects of truth.[139] Schematically, these are: truth as nature, truth as freedom, truth as mystery, and truth as participation. Under these four headings, Balthasar will outline an entire metaphysic, marrying the objectivity of scholastic thought to the concern of the great German philosophers (even though these go unnamed) for the inwardness of the knowing process. He seeks no less than to throw light on everything – from the way a plant inhabits its environment to human truth's openness to the truth of God – as he goes along.

Balthasar discusses his most basic concept of truth under the heading of *truth as nature.* That basic concept turns out to combine the Hellenic notion of truth as unveiledness or disclosure: in Greek, *alêtheia* (hence, truth as – in the widest possible sense – revelation) with the Hebraic concept of truth as fidelity: in Hebrew *emeth* (in this context, faithfulness to what may be disclosed.) Both features of the concept, especially when taken in tandem, ensure that central to Balthasar's treatment of truth as nature will be the relation between subject and object. Truth is when an object unveils itself to a subject who engages himself thereby in that disclosure. The relation between subject and object is a perennial topic in philosophy, of course, but one that acquires a fresh look here from the way it is introduced. Balthasar is enough of a Latin scholastic to want to insist that our knowledge is always measured by the sheer independent reality of things. But he is also enough of a classical Germanist to maintain with equal vigour that subjectivity is self-determining and creative. His resolution of the resultant *aporia* – the state we find ourselves in when thinking gets stuck in an impasse – follows from the foundational idea of truth with which he began. Authentic knowledge is as receptive to unveiling as it is sponta-

neous in its engaging fidelity. Human knowing is at once 'receptive and spontaneous, measured and measuring'[140]. It is
hospitality to the strange truth that, once welcomed, expands in
finding itself at home.

What this comes down to is that *things, when understood,
become more fully themselves.* Balthasar argues that the final
explanation of this state of affairs lies in the way things are
constituted as intelligible by the divine mind. It is because God
knows things that they are essentially knowable – including, of
course, knowable to us. Ultimately, the logic with which we are
operating as human beings is founded on divine creation. That is
why knowing has to embrace *both* the receptivity that tells us
that things are given to us *and* the spontaneity that prolongs the
Creator's act by so entertaining things as to make of them
something more. The co-discoverer of evolution by natural
selection, Alfred Russel Wallace, argued that the rationale of
colour-effects in, for example, butterfly wings and the plumage
of birds so exceeds the demands of 'utility' in biological nature
that we have to think – theistically – of evolution's proper
outcome as the distinctively human enjoyment of the 'greatest
show on earth'.

> To claim that the lower animals, especially the
> mammals, perceive all the shades and intensities,
> the contrasts and the harmonies of colours as we
> perceive them, and that they are affected as we
> are with their unequalled beauty is a wholly
> unjustified hypothesis.[141]

But of course we are not *compelled* to enjoy – or recreate in
photography or the arts – that 'unequalled beauty'. That we
sometimes do so belongs to what I termed above our 'hospitality' in knowing, and as that word suggests, it is an act of freedom
and therefore (compare Balthasar's exploration of the Good) an
'act of love'[142]. In a hidden manner, it is a way of answering the
call of God. By our awareness of the primordial 'measuring' of

things, which awaits our derivative 'measuring' for its full flow-
ering, a basic communication between God and ourselves is, for
Balthasar, already established.[143] This is one of the points in his
theological logic where he thinks through St Thomas' philosophy in a fresh way: the fundamental picture of human knowing
of things as depending on divine knowing of them had long since
been laid out by Aquinas in his *Disputed Questions on Truth*[144].

The issue of *truth as freedom* was inescapable against both
the German philosophical and the biblical background – not
least for the future author of a theological dramatics! The power
of self-manifestation is an echo of the divine freedom, even
when, as with sub-spiritual beings, the 'intimacy' a thing has is
limited, or even minimal. Still, to become an object of knowledge to others, to whatever degree, is a sharing of self, and
something of a service. Throughout the universe of being,
Balthasar hears echoes, faint or otherwise, of the *Hingabe* (self-
surrender) that is for him, as we saw in Chapter Three, the crux
of the triune life. He may seem to over-moralise the life of insect
or beast. But for Balthasar the contrast of such creatures with
man lies not in any lack of self-communication on the part of the
former but in the absence among them of the power to *witness*.
Witness is self-communication taken onto a new level.

But the will to self-communication on the part of the object
would be fruitless without a corresponding will to self-opening
on the part of the subject. It is only through the subject's freedom
that the object can achieve its potential there. This is most
conspicuously so in the case of communication between spiritual subjects when in inter-personal knowledge the truth
involved bears the character of intimacy (though Balthasar
stresses how for human, over against angelic, subjects, such
cognitive commerce remains incarnate, mediated through the
body). Some truth is only rationally accessible when it is communicated in freedom. Here above all, true knowledge is never
without an element of love.

> *Love is by no means on the far side of truth. It is*
> *that which, within truth, ensures an ever-new*

> *mystery over and above all unveiling; it is the*
> *eternal more-than-what-we–already-know*
> *without which there would be neither knowing*
> *nor knowable; it is that which, within the real,*
> *never permits a being to become a mere fact and*
> *never permits knowledge to rest on its laurels*
> *but makes it serve something higher still.*[145]

In pursuit of its role in 'logic', love is generous enough to admit every truth whatever its provenance. It is also clear-sighted enough to establish a hierarchy among the truths it knows. Above all, it can distinguish between a more comprehensive truth and one that is only included within a wider whole. All that is highly pertinent to a divine revelation (in Israel, Christ, the Church, and in their perspective, history and the cosmos) than which no greater truth can be conceived. We recall from Chapter One how the holism of revelation is for Balthasar a sign of its maximal expression of the transcendental 'unity', itself the mark of the indivisibility of beauty, goodness, and truth.

What of *truth as mystery?* Actually, Balthasar has touched on it already. In expounding aspects of truth, he has been advancing a general ontology of the real that opens out, like one throwing wide a casement, onto mystery. Thus, for example, in illustrating the object-subject relation, he considered how the world is a sign system with a meaning beyond itself. We're familiar with sign systems having a meaning within the world; why should there not be a meaning to the wider sign system of the world as a whole? Again, in discussing freedom, he had pondered the way in which essence and existence, those twin terms of all fundamental ontology, *what* something is and *that* it is, point to their 'common mystery', which is *being*. Something's essence, seen as its proper way of being, is more than what, at any given point, it actually is because, typically enough, a thing strives for the fullness of its own kind of life. And something's existence is not just brute fact, but depends on the victory, in its inmost constitution, of being over non-being. Now, however, Balthasar will be dealing with truth as mystery in so many words.

In a world of images, being comes to be interpreted by us. Its approach is delicate, as such errors as phenomenalism warn us. There is a 'kenotic', self-emptying side to its appearance, a distant reflection, Balthasar thinks, of the self-emptying of the divine Logos, in the manger at Bethlehem, his growth to maturity in Nazareth, his ministry in Galilee, and on the Cross – behind which lies the entire kenotic Trinity. This humble approach of being in the image often happens beautifully, for beauty is the power of expressive truth to radiate out and captivate. Balthasar employs the Aristotelian-Thomist philosophy of mind as 'abstractive' (i.e. drawing out from things their 'species' – the images in which the forms of things present themselves to us) in order to show how our concepts are shaped on this very basis.

But his analysis is in the service of a claim more distinctively his own. Through images, by way of concepts, the essences of things, which are indeed *manners* of being, stand revealed. But by the same token, this mediation brings home to us the range and depth of what is displayed by 'being' at large. We might well reflect on the frequent difficulty of an *immediate* grasp of the real, since, were it not so, we could rely wholly on common sense and would have nothing to learn from the sciences and arts. It takes all the arts and sciences, tutored by sound philosophy, to draw significance out.

This reminds Balthasar of the inescapable heuristic importance of language without which these disciplines and practices would either fail or (in the case, say, of sculpture or painting), be disabled. In human language, the environing world of images takes on a new role as a repertoire of forms that can be drawn on for the purposes of communication between human beings. By maximalising the possibilities not only of faithful but also of deceitful presentation of the world, language can scarcely be said to eliminate mystery. What it does do is make us attend to the importance of inter-subjectivity, of dialogue. Personal perspectives, drawing (inevitably) on the resources furnished by culture, are enriching – but each must be co-ordinated with the rest in the interests of gaining the largest view. Not, however, that this will ever, after the style of Hegelianism, abolish the point of the personal. If anything, says Balthasar, it shows the need for a communion of saints.

Balthasar's conclusion on the mystery of being is that, judged by its trace in the contingent order, the ground of things is a communicativeness that is marked by disinterestedness, by gratuity – and thus by something like love. The ground (the infinite, God in his gift of being) differs from the grounded (the finite, the creature in its reception of that gift) through not being determined by any factors beyond self. Like the world, God is in a sense groundless, but in an utterly different sense from that in which the world is groundless. The world, while indeed lacking a ground of its own, is actually grounded in another – in the divine gratuity, whereas God really is grounded in nothing but his own blessed life.

> *In revealing himself as the Creator, God shows*
> *that he is at once the deep source of the world*
> *and the absolutely hidden being. He unveils*
> *himself in the exact measure required for*
> *teaching the creature that he remains the*
> *Creator who is both free and hidden in his own*
> *mystery.*[146]

Hence: *truth as participation*. If what has just been said under the heading 'truth as mystery' explains why 'God and the world' can only be spoken of in the same breath by appeal to analogy, it also indicates how what is disclosure of hidden mystery from God's side can only be from our side participation in that act, never possession of it. And that in turn explains why the most important cognitive attitude we can ever adopt is one which awaits from God alone the measure of the truth we would know. Listening to the Word of God in Jesus Christ depends on this. We are not surprised to find that truth has a 'dramatic structure'[147], and so is crucially involved in the theo-drama whose chief protagonist Israel's Messiah is. This brings us to our next main topic.

The truth of the Word, the Son

In the second volume of the theological logic, natural logic, the ontology ('onto-logic') proper to the everyday – which is not say banal or commonplace – world, must become 'Christo-logic' by focusing on the Logos, and him incarnate, since it is through the Word incarnate that a revelation inviting man's fullest possible participation in being (what the New Testament calls 'everlasting life') actually occurred.[148] At the same time, the reader should beware. The second and third volumes of Balthasar's *Theo-logic*, though they presuppose the first, do not follow on it from it in direct or exclusive fashion. In between – both chronologically and argumentatively – there intervene the aesthetics and dramatics. Thus, when Balthasar opens his Christo-logic with a sustained meditation on the saying of the Christ of St John's Gospel, 'I am the Truth' (John 14:6), the intellectual shock, for readers moving straight to this point from 'Truth of the World', is barely tolerable. The picture looks very different, however, if our mind has been prepared by *The Glory of the Lord*, the main source for Balthasar's theological aesthetics, and *Theo-drama*, his chief presentation of theological dramatics, in the meanwhile. We shall be more willing to consider the central question of the second volume of *Theo-logic* – how could the eternal Logos express himself within the bounds of a creature, the humanity of Jesus? – if we have previously done two things. And these are: contemplate the self-disclosure of the divine glory in Jesus Christ, as found in the aesthetics; and, with the dramatics, confront the divine philanthropy where the same figure is the central protagonist of the divine action, transforming fallen finite freedom by joining it to all-holy infinite freedom in the sacrifice of the Cross. The aesthetics had already discovered, in the unfolding of the Word of the Cross through the scenes of Jesus' life, death and Resurrection, how God clarifies the form of his own truth as gracious, self-giving love. The dramatics spelled that out in terms of the action of Christ, in tears and blood.

But now, within a theological logic dedicated to the Son, one can take a step further. The splendid goodness of truth is uttered not only in the fateful career, up to Easter, of the Word made flesh, but also in the gift at Pentecost of a share in the entire relation between Father and Son, a gift communicated through the Holy Spirit. Balthasar signals clearly enough, as the second volume of *Theo-logic* opens, that the trilogy will not be able to end without a final volume, beyond Christology, on the truth of the Holy Spirit. As the Interpreter of the Son – who is himself the Interpreter of the invisible Father – the Spirit transmits to the world the gracious Truth of Father and Son not only exteriorly, as the Advocate defending the truth of Christian claims, but also interiorly, as the 'Anointing' spoken of in the First Letter of St John (2:20). The Spirit it is who gives believers a share in this relation between Father and Son in such wise that they may know that relation for themselves.

Despite such appeal to spiritual experience, Balthasar would deny he has left the realm of logic – the 'think' that 'thing' becomes – far behind. The first volume of *Theo-logic* had already argued that love plays an indispensable role in thought. Its second volume will argue the case for a human logic in the image and likeness of the triune God, the God of love. Logic and love, which some would regard as an ill-assorted couple, not to say polar opposites, can, after all, meet and embrace.

Ana-logic

I suppose one could paraphrase Balthasar's word 'ana-logic' by comparison with the movement of an escalator, and call it 'Logic Going Up'. 'Ana-logic' is Balthasar's term for enquiry into reflection of the Trinity in the truth and being of the world – which will mean, then, ways in which certain features of the world point upward to the transcendent triune God who is their source. That suggests the difference from 'analogy', a word otherwise close to Balthasar's neologism (confusingly so, some might say). Analogy *may* refer to the affinities between the world and God, but it doesn't have to. It can quite well concern itself exclusively with the family resemblance between things *within* the world – the 'healthy' character of a fruit-and-bran breakfast when compared with, say, the similarly 'healthy' tone of someone's skin. By contrast, 'ana-logic', as Balthasar uses the term, always looks from the world towards God. Balthasar means by it: reflection intended to throw light on the self-expression of the Logos (who is always, we recall, the *Trinitarian* Son) in his creation, analysing that self-expression *from the side of the world*.

This led Balthasar to become interested in triads. I can offer some examples. With the French poet-metaphysician Paul Claudel, Balthasar maintains that all logic has a triadic structure. No 'A' can be determined except by reference to an indefinite series of delimiting co-determinants, as also to an unlimited determinant without which there would be infinite regress. With a nod to a mediaeval Augustinian theologian, Richard of St Victor, he finds a triadic pattern also in personhood: no one can be a genuine person (as distinct from a mere individual) without inter-subjectivity, and in inter-subjective relations persons find each other in some common 'fruit', be it offspring, shared activity, or whatever. With help from twentieth century 'dialogical' thinkers, he finds the same triadic structure in language, where the truth that occurs in authentic speaking between some 'I' and 'some 'thou' requires its ultimate ground beyond the human two. These are ana-logical projection lines: in other words, traces of the Trinity in the structure of both thought and being in the world. But their point of intersection is unknown to us until the Logos takes flesh as Jesus Christ.

It is in Jesus Christ that the Word has expressed himself, by his visibility unveiling the actual structure of the divine life. Above all, this means knowledge of the Father, the Source of the entire Godhead. Here Balthasar cannot resist citing one of his favourite masters, Irenaeus:

> *Conformably to his majesty it is impossible to*
> *know God. It is not possible, then, that the*

> *Father be measured. But according to his love –*
> *for this love is that which, through his Word,*
> *shows us the way to God – we ever learn by*
> *obedience to him that God is the one who is thus*
> *great.*[149]

In Balthasar's general ontology, so we saw when considering 'Truth of the World', the more fully the mystery of being is disclosed in some striking appearance, the more we are aware of the unfathomable depths beneath. It may seem surprising, then, that he is so opposed to that distinction between divine energies (revealed) and divine essence (hidden) associated with the fourteenth-century Byzantine theologian St Gregory Palamas.[150] He prefers other ways of inculcating due reserve about the claim that heaven itself was opened in the Incarnation, notably in the way he treats the divine self-expression in the man Jesus and in his emphasis (a novel form of apophatic theology, this) on the silence of Christ.

As the parables and other sayings indicate, Jesus has at his disposal the 'grammar' of creation – that logic whose language is furnished by creaturely being as such – and the 'grammar' of Israel – the Hebrew Bible or Old Testament: two sets of linguistic resources, then, for speaking of the Father. Jesus entered as man a world – and a people – ana-logically prepared for him, ana-logically resourced for his purposes.

But in his manner of using these resources, and his entire deportment, Jesus is marked, so Balthasar reports, by an extraordinary *otherness* (this is no common creature, no ordinary Jew), even when engaged in his humble service of his fellows. Balthasar emphasises in this connexion how he speaks by silences. The silence of the prisoner before Caiaphas, Herod, and Pilate makes eloquent another, all-environing silence, which spans the time from the Incarnation itself to his return to the Father's side. Even – or especially – when making himself comprehensible, Jesus retains his mystery and his initiative. (Here we see why Balthasar regards the Palamite distinction as misguided: it locates the mystery in the wrong place.)

But speaking of places, what in any case is the place of the Logos in God? In a Christian theological account of the truth of God, Balthasar can hardly avoid offering a constructive dogmatics of the Holy Trinity. Nothing less is feasible if the aim is to exhibit the truth of one who is always the 'Trinitarian Son'. (Here you must bear, gentle reader, with a little technical Trinitarian theology.) Balthasar steers a course between radical 'essentialism' for which the Fatherly origin of Son and Spirit virtually coincides with the divine essence common to the hypostases, and radical 'personalism' for which it is not out of his substance, the unique divine being, that the Father is fecund but only out of his personhood, as he generates the Son and spirates the Spirit.[151] For Balthasar, the divine essence exists in a way that is never other than 'Fatherly, Sonly, Ghostly'. The essence is co-extensive with the event of the eternal processions of these persons. And it is co-determinative of that event by way of the – in each case, unique – participation in that essence of Father, Son, and Spirit. The self-giving of the persons corresponds, then, to the singularity of the essence, which in turn indicates that the intimate reality of the essence can only be *the being of love*.

> *If the self-giving of the Father to the Son and*
> *of both to the Spirit corresponds neither to a*
> *free arbitration nor to a necessity but to God's*
> *intimate Essence, then this most intimate*
> *Essence – however we may distinguish between the*
> *processions – can itself be in the last analysis*
> *only love.*[152]

Whereas some theologies of the Trinity want to replace the language of being with the language of love, Balthasar proposes that the gift of love shall illuminate being from within. As we had occasion to note in the last chapter, it is not Balthasar's way to contrast being with love. He is much too philosophical to be a sentimentalist. That does not prevent him, however, from being an out-and-out 'agapeist', a theologian of love. In Balthasar's account of the divine nature, all the divine properties take their coloration from what he terms 'the primordial mystery of abyssal love'[153].

If, within the divine life, the Son expresses the truth of the Father, he must by that very token manifest the Father's 'groundless' love. And so he does, within the Trinity, by his role in the coming forth of the Holy Spirit. On that disputed question between Orthodoxy and Catholicism, Balthasar is an unrepentant Filioquist: he holds, with the Catholic Church, that the Spirit proceeds from the Father *and the Son*.[154] In reading the Gospels, then, the logic of the Word incarnate cannot be reduced to 'Jesus-ism'. It must include Jesus' 'whence', the Father, and his 'whither', the Holy Spirit. It will not be possible to grasp the Son's work except in relation to the Father who sends him and whose reign he inaugurates, and to the Spirit in whom he himself is sent and whose gift he releases into the world.

In so saying, Balthasar anticipates the closing chapters of *Theo-logic*'s middle volume, concentrating as these do on the career of Jesus. But meanwhile he must treat of the role of the Logos in the world's making (rather than redeeming), the emergence of the world through the Word. A theology of the creative agency of the Word in the world's making will follow from an account of his particular way of sharing the divine essence as a person. Greek Christian thought always had difficulty showing the difference between Word and Spirit in their procession from the Father. It was, in part, to differentiate their origins that Augustine launched the enormously successful analogy of the Word as intellectual movement, *Verbum*, the Spirit as movement of love, *Amor*.

Balthasar, however, prefers to take his cue here not from Augustine (and Thomas after him) but from Thomas' Franciscan contemporary, Bonaventure, who developed the Augustinian inheritance somewhat differently. For Bonaventure – and Balthasar accepts this – both Word and Spirit proceed from the Father's love, but the Word proceeds 'expressively', by expression of the Father, while the Spirit proceeds 'liberally', by his readiness to be sent into the world as the boundless overflow of the Father's generosity expressed in the Son. Hence the readiness of the Word to serve as exemplar for the world's being in its complex unity, for this is the world's expression of the divine ideas of things, the world's being in its own way divinely expressive too). And hence the Word's willingness to take on the nature of that creature who, made in the God's image, enjoys the closest relationship of being with the Logos that creation affords. Namely, ourselves: humankind, who are made in God's image and likeness.

Natural philosophy, like the human sciences, shows us a diverse creation blessed with difference yet cursed by conflict. For Balthasar, recapitulating here not only the early discussion of the distinction between essence and existence in the first volume of *Theo-Logic* but the far fuller account in the metaphysics volume of *The Glory of the Lord*, this distinction sets creatures off as finite, at the other pole from the God who is infinite. It thus signals not only their poverty but also their glory, for in their multiform contingency (in all their variety, none of them *had to* be), we see how being reflects the kenotic divine Trinity by gloriously throwing itself away.[155] This confirms what the theological dramatics had to say, in the way they dealt with the freedom of God, as described in Chapter Two. How Balthasar sees, with Bonaventure, the coming forth from the Father of the Word and the Spirit of the one God also gives useful support to the conclusions of the dramatics on 'otherness' as well. Otherness – whether invoked in contrast to God or to each other – is no stranger to the triune being where the persons are defined by their relations of *fruitful and responsive* opposition. There is nothing preordained about the link *we* see between difference and conflict, otherness and competition.

And indeed the Bonaventurian theology of the divine processions in the second volume of *Theo-logic* sheds some retrospective light on the whole approach to Christian theology recommended by Balthasar when he built his house of thought on the transcendentals – compare my introductory chapter in the present book. Finite as is the manner of the transcendentals – the true, the beautiful, the good – in creation, they nonetheless signal a share in the Trinitarian expressivity (like the Son) and liberality (like the Holy Spirit).

Cata-logic

If 'ana-logic' is the elevator ascending, Logic Going Up, 'cata-logic' is Balthasar's term for the descending movement whereby through his Incarnation God brings a new quality of being, a new ontology, into the world: Logic Coming Down. 'Cata-logic' is Balthasar-speak for the way, in his descent into the world, the Word resolves discord into harmony and brings about a recon-ciled creation. Christ comes as Word incarnate to fulfil the work the Trinity enterprised from the beginning of the world.

Balthasar's concept of this is very generous, and draws on a number of his predecessors in the great Tradition. The incarnate Word unifies tensions in cosmic being, creating equilibrium between what in us is ultra-particular or hyper-universal. He unifies the arts and sciences, being as he is a principle that can order the intellectual space they inhabit. He unifies history, furnishing the key to the significance of its process. He unifies the world with God, acting as a medium between the two.

For classical Christianity this last point has always been central. Balthasar's emphasis lines on the happening of the 'at-one-ment' (of God and the world) *in the flesh*. For theologi-cal aesthetics, the flesh – the sensuous realm – had been the pivot. For theological dramatics, though the flesh was in itself no sinful principle, in history it had turned away from the life of God that is the light of men. To restore its integrity was why the Word assumed it. Now in the theological logic, the stress will lie on the potential for redemptive expression found in the union of finite flesh and infinite Word.

The 'language' of flesh is the language of man as a spiritual-corporeal unity. Accordingly, the language of faith has many registers. The language of sounds and words is itself but the highest instance of natural revelatory and communicative expressiveness. So prior to dealing with exclusively linguistic modes, Balthasar treats the expression of the Word made flesh in terms of myth and icon. In the Incarnation, myth became fact (shades of C. S. Lewis on the same topic, as I already had occasion to mention in Chapter Two).

> *The Trinitarian God is ... no subsequently*
> *excogitated dogma, but manifests himself in*
> *immediate fashion in the fact of the Word*
> *made flesh.*[156]

In that Incarnation an 'icon' of divine Personhood was fashioned in the human face of Christ. In Jesus we have an objective symbol of God, and one who, in his own speech, uses parables that take us beyond their inevitable finitude towards inexhaustible transcendence. But all the many words Jesus spoke, and the many states through which he passed in life, are so many modulations of his being the eternal Word, that is, the Father's self-expression, and hence the embodiment of charity.

In the end, however, Jesus is rejected, and the Word is contradicted – theologically extraordinary, for then a lie must assert its truth in the presence of Truth itself. But this Truth is the disclosure of absolute love: so Jesus the Word is rejected not only through error but also by sin. The dialectic in the ministry involves not only Jesus' argumentative opponents but also, and more profoundly, the contrary forces of evil. It is overcome by the persevering obedience to the Father of the Logos made human, an obedience that finds its climax on the Cross and in the Descent into Hell. The outcome of the theo-logical clash is the victory of Christ when, serenely entrusting to God the collapse of his earthly work, Jesus allows that work to develop beyond himself, in the sphere of the Resurrection 'administered' – stewarded – by the Holy Spirit. And it is the Spirit's truth we must now in conclusion consider if we are to do a Christian logic justice.

The truth of the Holy Spirit

It is the Holy Spirit who interprets the incarnate Son as Son of the Father: hence his 'entry into logic'[157]. Balthasar makes approving reference to Hegel's comment in the *Lectures on the Philosophy of Religion* that whereas, before Pentecost, the disciples had already known Christ, they had not yet known him *as infinite truth*. This is the difference the Spirit makes.

To know Christ according to the Spirit is impossible without receiving the Spirit. And as the Fathers of the fourth century saw, this makes no sense unless the Spirit is himself God.[158] Balthasar's version of their classic argument for the truth of the Spirit is: how can One who expounds the truth of the Son's revelation of the Father not himself be divine?

In the first instance, then, the Holy Spirit enters a theological logic in that guise in which the Jesus of the High Priestly Prayer in St John's Gospel presents him as one who will 'lead the disciples into all truth' (John 16:13). Balthasar emphasises the holistic nature of the task this allots the third Person. The Spirit is to bring to light and life not so much particular aspects of revelation for their own sake but, rather, for the way those aspects give access to revelation as a totality. As Balthasar puts it, severely, a theology that loses itself in particulars, or a 'praxis' (a form of practice of the Christian faith) that brings unilaterally into prominence some one aspect of Christianity, cannot lay claim to animation by the Spirit. To make available all the treasures of wisdom and knowledge that lie hidden in Christ Jesus: this is the heart of the 'economy' of the Holy Spirit, his contribution to the Christian dispensation. Without the 'qualitative catholicity' of that holistic grasp of revelation, the Church will be poorly equipped for the pursuit of 'quantitative catholicity' – for carrying the gospel of Christ to the ends of the earth. Balthasar was always worried by catholicity being sold short – something he found happening time and again through reductionism in the Church after the Second Vatican Council (as also, by a certain sclerosis of the imagination, in the Church before that Council).[159] Here Balthasar signals that much of the third volume of *Theo-logic* devoted to the Spirit will be given over to ecclesiology, the investigation of the *Church* of the Spirit.

Though Balthasar by no means neglects the causal agency of the Spirit in the mission of Christ, his emphasis, in the context of theological logic, lies with the Spirit as Interpreter, or, as he often writes, 'Exegete', in the Church. True, it is the Spirit who, from the first moment of Jesus' conception, has rendered his humanity obedient to the mission the Son received from the Father. Contrary to what Filioquist doctrine might lead one to conjecture, in the special circumstances of the economy, the Son allows the Spirit to carry him forward on the Father's project of redemption. Still, so far as the disciples are concerned, the Spirit is a kind of second gift bestowed for the more effective appreciation of the first gift made us by the Father in sending his Son.

> *How can an historical person claim universal*
> *validity? ... This dilemma is only soluble in a*
> *Trinitarian way, and, to be more precise,*
> *pneumatologically. The Father works not*
> *with one hand alone but with two.*[160]

That 'more effective appreciation' of Jesus Christ is made possible by the love the Holy Spirit sheds abroad in our hearts. Thus the role of the Spirit in the post-Pentecost economy reflects his place in the inner-Trinitarian life, where he is from all eternity the living, personal gift of Father and Son rounding off the being of the Trinity as love.

A theological logic is concerned with salvation's intelligible structure – not its attractive radiance, which belongs to theological aesthetics, nor its power to resolve life's conflicts in favour of the good, the subject matter of theological dramatics. In this perspective, Balthasar speaks of the Spirit as 'expounding' a two-fold movement – from Father to Son in the Incarnation and from Son to Father in the Resurrection of the Crucified. What the Spirit lays out in so doing is the definitive revelation of the

Father in the former, the endless glory of the Son in the latter, and in both the perfection of their mutual love. The share of disciples in this movement and disclosure is what the Greeks call 'divinisation'; and the Latins 'incorporation in Christ'. These are for Balthasar complementary schemes which exhibit the Spirit and the Son working together as (in a favoured metaphor from St Irenaeus) the 'two hands' of the Father.[161] Under this rubric, by way of exploration, then, of the mutually defining character of the economies of the Son and Spirit, Balthasar will illuminate a variety of theological topics: the relation of theory to 'praxis'; the nature of Christian experience; the historically concrete yet universally valid claims of revelation.

The Spirit (this is the upshot of these discussions) never renders the Word discarnate. On the contrary! It is when the Son undergoes Incarnation to the uttermost, in the final sufferings on the Tree of the Cross, that the Spirit most completely penetrates his manhood. From this Balthasar draws a law of Christian living. 'Pneumaticisation' always increases in direct proportion to 'Incarnation'. It is an axiom highly pertinent to the account of the Church that follows. No Church that would be exclusively spiritual and subjective and not at all corporeal and objective in its manner of proceeding could possibly be the continuing Spirit-borne presence of Jesus Christ.

The Holy Spirit, Balthasar argues, is not only the personal love of Father and Son, the expression of their inter-subjectivity. He is also supremely objective, the fruit of their love. This duality has ecclesiological consequences. He is not only the Spirit who inspires sanctity in human subjects, initiating prayer and pardon, granting mystical and charismatic gifts, and the capacity of individuals to bear witness to Christ.[162] All of that – 'subjective Spirit', Balthasar calls it, in a play of words (and concepts) drawn from Hegel's *Phenomenology* – he most certainly is. But the Spirit also inspires such outer forms and institutional mediations of the saving revelation as Tradition, Scripture, Church office, preaching, the liturgy and sacraments, and even canon law and theology. All of this – 'objective Spirit' –

is also he. What, on the basis of Christ's founding activity, the Spirit constructs in the Church's institution is as much the expression of the divine love as is the holiness that the pattern of the Church's life makes possible. Balthasar, then, writes a pro-mystical ecclesiology which is also, and equally, an anti-Gnostic one. The Church is Marian, having its being through participating in Mary's unlimited faith, hope, and love. It is also Petrine, founded on sacrament and ministerial succession in all their definiteness.[163]

The goal of both subjective and objective Spirit is return to the Father's house, and this is so not for individuals only but for the story of the world.[164] All portrayals of the Source and Goal in world religion are but 'schematisms', unsatisfying philosophical abstractions, if they fail to realise that God's being is love, both absolutely in itself, and economically, in its outpouring in the free gift of the Son for our fetching home. The trilogy will not end in baffled cessation of thought before Truth's final mystery. Divine love has opened itself to knowledge, but knowledge, for its part, must

> *stay open to the marvel of a love issuing eternally from itself, without other ground, without further reason.*[165]

Pondering the divine Logic should change not only our minds but our hearts. Ultimately – or so, with the early Romantic poet Novalis (his real name was Friedrich Leopold von Hardenberg), Balthasar wished his readers to respond: 'Desire for a strange land has left us; We want to go home to the Father'. Secular-minded critics, both outside and inside the Church, may not like our saying so, but that is where humankind is meant to belong.

---

[133] An earlier version of this Chapter appeared as 'The Theo-Logic' in E. T. Oakes, S. J., and D. Moss (ed.), *The Cambridge Companion to Hans Urs von Balthasar* (Cambridge, Cambridge University Press, 2004), pp. 159–171.

[134] P. Blättler, *Pneumatologia crucis. Das Kreuz in der Logik von Wahrheit und Freiheit. Ein phänomenologischer Zugang der Theologik Hans Urs von Balthasars* (Würzburg, Echter, 2004), pp. 22, 23.

135 The theme of Karl Joseph Wallner's study *Gott als Eschaton. Trinitarische Dramatik als Voraussetzung göttlicher Universalität bei Hans Urs von Balthasar* (Vienna, Heiligenkreuzer Verlag, 1992).

136 This is how Wolfgang Klaghofer-Treitler explains the inter-relation of the first to the second and third parts of Balthasar's *Theologik* in his *Karfreitag. Auseinandersetzung mit Hans Urs von Balthasars 'Theologik'* (Innsbruck-Vienna, Tyrolia Verlag, 1997), pp. 16–69. It is the obvious way to read the differentiated unity of this work.

137 *Wahrheit. Wahrheit der Welt* (Einsiedeln, Johannes Verlag, 1947).

138 *Mein Werk. Durchblicke* (Einsiedeln, Johannes Verlag, 1990), p. 24.

139 I follow now his own account in *Theo-logic: Theological Logical Theory I. Truth of the World* (San Francisco, Ignatius, 2000). References will be, however, to the German original since the American translation of *Theologik* is not readily accessible to me.

140 *Theologik I. Wahrheit der Welt* (Einsiedeln, Johannes Verlag, 1985), p. 34.

141 M. A. Flannery (ed.), *Alfred Russel Wallace's Theory of Intelligent Evolution* (Riesel, TX, Erasmus Press, 2008), pp. 122–123.

142 *Theologik I. Wahrheit der Welt*, op. cit., p. 76.

143 The most potent form of this communication is when we ponder our own 'measuring', the 'given' that awaits our personal re-appropriation as we seek to make something of ourselves: in Balthasar's memorable axiom, *Cogitor ergo sum*, 'I am thought, therefore I am'.

144 Thomas Aquinas, *Quaestiones disputatae de Veritate*, q. 22, a. 2, ad i.

145 *Theologik I. Wahrheit der Welt*, op. cit., p. 118.

146 A. Nichols, O. P., *Say it is Pentecost*, op. cit., p. 56.

147 D. C. Schindler, *Hans Urs von Balthasar and the Dramatic Structure of Truth* (New York, Fordham University Press, 2001).

148 *Theo-logic. Theological Logical Theory II. Truth of God* (San Francisco, Ignatius, 2004).

149 Irenaeus, *Adversus haereses IV. 20. 1*, cited in *Theologik II. Wahrheit Gottes* (Einsiedeln, Johannes Verlag, 1985), p. 63. The case has been made that Balthasar's entire theological project is an exercise in Neo-Irenaeanism: thus K. Mongrain, *The Systematic Theology of Hans Urs von Balthasar: an Irenaean Retrieval* (New York, Continuum, 2002). That cannot be said, however, without somewhat downplaying other sources – and Mongrain is especially inclined to underestimate the contribution of Balthasar's mystical associate, Adrienne von Speyr.

150 Interest in Palamism, somewhat neglected for centuries, revived in Orthodoxy thanks especially to later nineteenth-century Russian scholars and is now an almost universal feature of Orthodox theology: I attempt an adjudication of the issues in 'John Meyendorff and Neo-Palamism', in A. Nichols, O. P., *Light from the East. Authors and Themes in Orthodox Theology* (London, Sheed and Ward, 1995), pp. 41–56.

151 I make (I hope, correctly) the same kind of claim for the Trinitarian theology of St Thomas in A. Nichols, O. P., *Discovering Aquinas. An Introduction to his Life, Work and Influence* (London, Darton, Longman and Todd, 2002), pp. 60–71. Though the premier student of these matters, Gilles Emery, O. P.,

is inclined to call the question, 'Essentialism or Personalism?' an 'ill-posed' one, he reverts to its terms when he writes that, while the 'constitution and subsistence of the [Triune] persons' is a matter of 'relationship in its integral being', we should not 'refuse to the essence the foundational role our grasp of the mystery assigns it'. Thus his 'Essentialisme ou personalisme dans le traité de Dieu chez saint Thomas d'Aquin?', *Revue Thomiste* 98 (1998), pp. 5–38.

[152] *Theologik II. Wahrheit Gottes*, op. cit., pp. 126–127.

[153] Ibid., p. 128.

[154] For an attempt to resolve this long-standing disputed question between Rome and the Orthodox, see A. Nichols, O. P., *Rome and the Eastern Churches. A Study in Schism* (San Francisco, Ignatius, 2010, 2nd edition), pp. 251–269.

[155] This explains why in that volume Balthasar can regard the self-abandonment of the saints in the spirituality of the Baroque age as a compensation for the decline of a right metaphysics in the same epoch: I develop this point in my essay 'Von Balthasar's Aims in his Theological Aesthetics', *Heythrop Journal* XL (1999), pp. 409–423.

[156] *Theologik II. Wahrheit Gottes*, op. cit., p. 272.

[157] *The Spirit of Truth. Theological Logical Theory* (San Francisco, Ignatius, 2005).

[158] See especially St Basil's treatise *On the Holy Spirit* (Crestwood, NY, Saint Vladimir's Press, [1980] 1997).

[159] Compare in this regard, two little works: on the post-Conciliar epoch, *In the Fullness of Faith. On the Centrality of the Distinctively Catholic* (San Francisco, Ignatius, 1988), and, on the pre-Conciliar epoch, *The Razing of the Bastions. On the Church in this Age* (San Francisco, Ignatius, 1993).

[160] *Theologik III. Der Geist der Wahrheit* (Einsiedeln, Johannes Verlag, 1987), p. 180.

[161] Irenaeus, *Adversus haereses IV. 7. 4.*

[162] Balthasar's concern with the mystical life in the Church was not confined to the Carmelite women and Adrienne von Speyr, as is shown by his choice of contribution to the series of German commentaries on the *Summa theologiae* of St Thomas. He elected Thomas's presentation of the charisms and the contemplative and active lives, which appeared as Volume 23 of the *Deutsche Thomas-Ausgabe* in 1954. There is a useful survey, but confining itself to works already in English, in C. Lee, 'The Role of Mysticism within the Church as Conceived by Hans Urs von Balthasar', in *Communio* 16 (1989), pp. 105–126.

[163] There is a wonderful discussion of this in Balthasar's essay 'Who is the Church?', found in *Spouse of the Word, Explorations in Theology II* (San Francisco, Ignatius, 1991), pp. 143–191.

[164] Hans Ottmar Meuffels takes this as his theme in *Einbergung des Menschen in das Mysterium der dreieinigen Liebe. Eine trinitarische Anthropologie nach Hans Urs von Balthasar* (Würzburg, Echter, 1991).

[165] *Theologik III. Der Geist der Wahrheit*, op. cit., pp. 406–407.

Conclusion

Looking back on the whole project, not only of the theological logic but of the thought surveyed in this short study as a whole, we can scan our original key-word, 'being', much more fully than we could at the beginning. Then it seemed that the constellation of the transcendentals gave us our fullest *entrée* to the mystery of being. Now, however, we can say far more. 'Being' is not understood aright save in the light of the Trinity, the truth of the Word and the Spirit as pointing us to the truth of the Father. For, in the words of a German commentator on Balthasar's great work, being

> is more proximately the likeness of the triune God, in that it
> reflects the unity of the self-being (*it is complete and simple*)
> *and self-giving* (*but it is also non-subsistent*) of the three
> Persons ...

adding, so as to remind us that nowhere else can we discover this but in the life, death and Resurrection of Christ, 'as this is carried out in the sending of Jesus'.[166] In the divine plan, moreover, being is a communion which will embrace – we hope – all the world.[167] Being and love – love and logic – are already one in God. Balthasar's hope was that they will also be one in us.

The reaction Balthasar hoped for from readers of his enquiry into 'the true' was not so much intellectual satisfaction at a conceptual system (he approved of totality-thinking in theology but not of 'systematics'). Rather, the gain he wished for them was deeper discipleship. The same could be said when the purpose is asked of his explorations of 'the beautiful' and 'the good'. That is hardly surprising. The same content found as logic in the exploration of the True, is contemplated as form in the exploration of the Beautiful, and acted out in freedom in the exploration of the Good. This is why holiness is the goal of Balthasar's theological work, and prayer (faith, hope, and charity, turned towards their Source) its pre-condition.

The main aim of this short study has been to offer a way in to Balthasar's vast and sometimes unwieldy corpus, and notably the trilogy which is its literary heart. The key-words I chose – 'being' for this project as a whole, 'form' for the theological aesthetics, 'freedom' for the theological dramatics, and (with startling unoriginality!) 'logic' for the theological logic – have, I hope, sufficiently proved their utility.

There also emerged, in my own mind, a secondary aim. It concerns what the end of an earlier paragraph of this short Conclusion called the 'goal' and the 'pre-condition' of theology in Balthasar's eyes. May there be something in these pages inspirational enough to encourage readers to holiness and to steady them in the praying life that flows from the theological virtues. That for him, after all, was the best test of whether any book was worthwhile.

---

[166] M. Bieler, 'Meta-anthropology and Christology: On the Philosophy of Hans Urs von Balthasar', *Communio* 20 (1993), p. 140, where I have translated from Latin the phrases in parenthesis, which come from a Scholastic philosophy (*'completum et simplex', 'sed non subsistens'*) to whose representatives it probably would not have occurred to construe them in such theological (Trinitarian and Christological) terms.
[167] Hence the sub-title of Nicholas Healy's study: *The Eschatology of Hans Urs von Balthasar. Being as Communion*, of which use was made in Chapter Three.

Index of Names